ACCOUNTING STANDARDS AND INTERNATIONAL FINANCE

ACCOUNTING STANDARDS AND INTERNATIONAL FINANCE

With Special Reference to Multinationals

Joseph M. Burns

American Enterprise Institute for Public Policy Research
Washington, D.C.

Joseph M. Burns is deputy director of monetary research, Office of Assistant Secretary for International Affairs, U.S. Department of the Treasury.

657. 9
B 967a

ISBN 0-8447-3225-7

Domestic Affairs Study 49, September 1976

Library of Congress Catalog Card No. 76-40618

Printed in the United States of America 78-3532

There are so many men who can figure costs,
and so few who can measure values.

San Marino, Calif. *Tribune*
(reprinted in *Reader's Digest*, August 1974)

Uncertainty and Expectation
are the joys of life.

Congreve, *Love For Love*
(quoted in J. R. Hicks, *Value and Capital*)

CONTENTS

PREFACE

This study of the interrelationship of accounting standards and international finance was prepared during the author's service as deputy director of monetary research, Office of Assistant Secretary for International Affairs, U.S. Treasury Department. The views expressed herein are solely those of the author and are not to be attributed to the U.S. Treasury Department.

This essay is an expansion of a paper that I presented at the American Enterprise Institute–Treasury Conference on Exchange Rate Flexibility, April 20–22, 1976. The earlier version covered Chapters 1 and 2 and the last two sections of Chapter 3 of the present essay.

In the course of this study, I have been aided materially by discussions with Robert Aliber, Gunter Dufey, and my Treasury colleagues Thomas Willett, John Rutledge, and Charles Pigott, as well as with Jules Cassel, Donald Kirk, Marvin Kosters, Rita Rodriguez, Wilson Schmidt, and Alva Way. Useful comments were also made by participants in seminars at the University of Chicago and the University of Michigan. I particularly wish to thank Milton Friedman and Harry G. Johnson for their insightful comments and for their encouraging the expansion of my conference paper. And I owe a debt of gratitude to my secretary, Shirley Bryant, for her efficient handling of the manuscript.

Washington, D.C.   Joseph M. Burns
June 1976

INTRODUCTION

Existing accounting standards have been coming under increasing attack. The criticism has typically not been directed at the logic of the rulings by the Financial Accounting Standards Board or its predecessor, the Accounting Principles Board. Rather, the criticism has in general been directed at the relevance or realism of the rulings.[1] Indeed, the reliance on generally accepted accounting principles, and consequently the use of historical cost data, has become a source of great concern in the current environment of inflation and price uncertainty.[2]

In an ideal state of accounting, all assets and liabilities—financial or nonfinancial—would be reported at their current value in end-of-period reporting statements (with an adjustment by a general price index where appropriate).[3] With such a system of accounting—economic value accounting—there would always be a perfect correspondence between accounting data and economic values.

Needless to say, for some assets and liabilities, this concept of accounting—economic value accounting—would be very difficult to implement. In particular, for fixed assets and inventories, *inter alia*, conceptual problems as well as measurement problems would exist. These problems are the primary reason why historical cost accounting for some items has persisted for so long.

---

[1] See, for example, Robert R. Sterling, "Relevant Financial Reporting in an Age of Price Changes," *Journal of Accountancy*, vol. 139, no. 2 (February 1975).

[2] For an analysis of the nature of our current environment of inflation and price uncertainty, see Benjamin Klein, "Our New Monetary Standard: The Measurement and Effects of Price Uncertainty, 1880–1973," *Economic Inquiry*, vol. 13, no. 4 (December 1975).

[3] Cf. Sterling, "Relevant Financial Reporting in an Age of Price Changes."

Under existing accounting standards, accounting (or reported) values are not necessarily the same as the economic values to which the data correspond. Furthermore, and of greater significance, the expected accounting values are not necessarily the same as the expected economic values to which the data correspond. Indeed, as this study points out, it would be fortuitous if these values were the same. This discrepancy between accounting data and economic values (on both a realized and expected basis) is likely to have some serious consequences—for the individual firm as well as for the national and international economic scene.

For the firm, the discrepancy between accounting and economic values induces corporate managers to make wrong (nonoptimal) decisions for the firm. In addition, it impairs the ability of corporate directors to exercise effective control over the corporation. As is pointed out, the introduction or enlargement of a discrepancy between accounting and economic values by accounting standards—such as the new standards for multinationals—thus induces corporate managers to alter their decision making away from their optimal plan.

For the international economy, investment by multinationals has likely been curtailed as a result of the new standards and the allocation of resources for a given volume of investment has been distorted. In addition, a bias has been introduced against a floating rate system. As is pointed out, this bias is unfortunate in view of the greater benefits that multinationals realize under floating rates than they do under an adjustable peg system of fixed rates.

The economic cost of discrepancies between accounting data and economic values has become increasingly burdensome in our current environment of inflation and price uncertainty. This paper examines this economic cost in the context of existing accounting standards with special reference to the new accounting standards for the reporting of foreign currency positions by multinational companies. The analysis and implications of the paper, however, extend beyond the particular standards in question.

Chapter 1 of this paper examines some background material on the new accounting standards for multinationals. Chapter 2 analyzes the probable economic effects of existing accounting standards, with special reference to the new standards. Chapter 3 examines the implications of fixed and floating rate systems for the uncertainty facing multinationals and their behavior. In addition, it discusses problems for multinationals and for floating rates that were created by the new accounting standards as well as some implications of these problems for public policy. Chapter 4 offers some concluding observations.

The principal conclusions of this paper are these: (1) The new accounting standards appear to have caused some serious economic problems. (2) The new system, with its uniformity of treatment, may nevertheless be preferable—in certain respects—to the old system which permitted numerous standards to exist simultaneously. (3) The new standards are not capricious, but—taken as a whole—are rather carefully based on generally accepted accounting principles. (4) Some of the generally accepted accounting principles appear to be outmoded in our current environment of inflation and price uncertainty. (5) The introduction of economic value accounting appears to be the only way of mitigating the problems arising under existing accounting standards.

There are many difficult practical problems associated with economic value accounting. Despite the difficulties, and despite the fact that we are living in an age of uncertainty (indeed, largely because we are living in such an age), it would be preferable to have figures which are reasonably accurate rather than to continue the use of figures which are assuredly wrong.

1
THE NEW ACCOUNTING STANDARDS FOR MULTINATIONALS

In October 1975, the Financial Accounting Standards Board (FASB) issued a statement *(Statement No. 8)* establishing standards for the reporting of, *inter alia*, foreign currency positions by multinational companies. The new standards have been viewed with concern by many multinationals and have attracted considerable attention, mostly unfavorable, in the press. The standards have in fact drawn more criticism than any other ones issued by the three-year-old FASB.[1]

This chapter examines some background material on the new accounting standards: the factors prompting the adoption of the new standards (section 1), the FASB's decisions that have generated the greatest controversy (section 2), and the rationale for the translation method that was adopted (section 3).

1. Factors Prompting the New Standards

The recent rulings by the Financial Accounting Standards Board (FASB) were prompted by three factors: expansion of business activities abroad by U.S. companies, extensive currency realignments, and the use of significantly different methods by different corporations for reporting foreign currency transactions and positions.[2]

---

[1] See, for example, "Alice in Accountingland," *Forbes*, April 15, 1975, pp. 37-38; "Learning to Live with Currency Fluctuations," *Business Week*, January 26, 1976; and "Focus on Balance Sheet Reform," *Business Week*, June 7, 1976. Several corporations have in fact urged the board to rescind its recommendations. Probably in response, the FASB "formally decided that it wouldn't reconsider its controversial pronouncement." (*Wall Street Journal*, April 29, 1976, p. 19.)

[2] See Financial Accounting Standards Board, *Statement of Financial Accounting Standards No. 8: Accounting for the Translation of Foreign Currency Transactions and Foreign Currency Financial Statements* (Stamford, Connecticut: Finan-

The use of different accounting methods meant that equally efficient companies in identical circumstances and with identical behavior might in fact report different levels of earnings, and that companies with different levels of efficiency but in identical circumstances and with identical behavior might report similar earnings. With common standards of accounting, the reported earnings of firms might well be more meaningful to the users of such data, including investors, creditors, and government officials.[3]

2. The FASB's Most Controversial Decisions

To achieve a uniform standard of accounting, the FASB had to make a number of important decisions. Those that have generated the greatest controversy appear to be (1) the appropriate exchange rate to use for the translation of certain balance sheet items of foreign subsidiaries for end-of-period reporting statements: fixed assets, inventories, and long-term debt denominated in a foreign currency; and (2) whether the gains or losses produced by changes in exchange rates should be recognized currently or amortized over a period of time.

Many methods for the translation of balance sheet items had been in use. Conceptually, three may be distinguished: the current–noncurrent method, the monetary–nonmonetary method, and the modified monetary–nonmonetary method.[4]

The current–noncurrent method generally translated current assets and liabilities at the current exchange rate and noncurrent assets and liabilities at applicable historical rates (that is, the rate in effect when the asset was acquired or the liability incurred). This method was originally used by almost all U.S. companies, and was still employed by a large number at the time when *Statement No. 8* was issued by the FASB.

The monetary–nonmonetary method generally translated monetary assets and liabilities at the current exchange rate and nonmonetary assets and liabilities at applicable historical rates.[5] This

---

cial Accounting Standards Board, October 1975). Hereafter, this publication is referred to as *Statement No. 8*.

[3] Cf. ibid.

[4] See M. Edgar Barrett and Leslie L. Spero, "Accounting Determinants of Foreign Exchange Gains and Losses," *Financial Analysts Journal*, vol. 31, no. 2 (March–April 1975), pp. 26–30; and Financial Accounting Standards Board, *Statement No. 8*.

[5] For translation purposes, assets and liabilities are monetary if they are expressed in terms of a fixed number of foreign currency units. All other balance sheet items are classified as nonmonetary. See Financial Accounting Standards Board, *Statement No. 8*.

method was also widely used by U.S. companies and was becoming increasingly popular.

A modified monetary–nonmonetary method allowed for the translation of inventory, along with monetary assets, at the current exchange rate. This method also had been used by many U.S. companies.[6]

The second controversy, which was related to the first one, was the time period in which recognition should be given to the gains or losses produced by the translation of balance sheet items at current exchange rates. Some companies had recognized the gains or losses as part of current earnings. Others had set up reserve accounts in the owners' equity portion of the balance sheet. For a few companies, the use of these reserve accounts meant that exchange gains or losses almost completely bypassed the income statement. Reserve accounts were started with exchange rate gains (from the translation of balance sheet items) that did appear on income statements. Additions to this account were made with unrealized gains, and deductions were made in the case of unrealized losses produced by exchange rate changes, but these subsequent additions and deductions did not appear on income statements. More often, however, companies used a reserve account to amortize unrealized exchange rate gains or losses over a period of years, with the period usually related to the expected life of the relevant item on the balance sheet.

The Decisions. The Financial Accounting Standards Board adopted a method of translation that is, in effect, very similar to the monetary–nonmonetary one described above. In addition, the FASB required that the gains or losses from exchange rate revaluations of assets and liabilities must be reported on a current basis. The new standards became effective for fiscal years beginning on or after January 1, 1976, with earlier application encouraged.

3. The Rationale for the Translation Method Adopted

Statement No. 8 establishes, *inter alia*, standards for the translation into U.S. dollars of foreign currency financial statements of U.S. subsidiaries abroad. One purpose of the translation is to consolidate the balance sheets of foreign subsidiaries with those of the parent U.S. company. To carry out this consolidation, the FASB ruled that the foreign statements—covering assets and liabilities most of which

---

[6] Cf. Barrett and Spero, "Accounting Determinants of Foreign Exchange Gains and Losses."

are denominated in the local currency—must first be prepared in conformity with generally accepted accounting principles in the United States. Then, the statements are to be translated into U.S. dollars by a method that does not alter the measurement bases—in order to preserve the generally accepted accounting principles.[7] The board recognized that the effects of this method of translation might not be consistent with the effects of exchange rate changes.[8]

The method of translation adopted by the FASB is known as the temporal method. According to this method, if an asset or liability is valued on a current basis (at spot or future prices), a current exchange rate is used for translation; whereas if an asset or liability is valued at historical cost, the historical exchange rate (that is, the exchange rate existing at the time of acquisition or issuance) is used for translation.

For fixed assets and inventories, the logical implications of the temporal method and the specific rulings of the FASB coincide perfectly. The temporal method requires fixed assets to be translated at historical exchange rates, since fixed assets are evaluated at historical

---

[7] In discussing the objectives of translation, the Financial Accounting Standards Board stated, "Remeasuring in dollars the assets, liabilities . . . measured or denominated in foreign currency should not affect . . . the measurement bases for assets and liabilities . . . otherwise required by generally accepted accounting principles. That is, translation should change the *unit of measure* [italics, FASB] without changing accounting principles." (*Statement No. 8*, paragraph 6, pp. 3-4.)

In Appendix D, "Basis for Conclusion," the FASB stated, "After considering the alternatives, the Board concluded that it should require the concept that has been implicitly understood and applied in practice, namely, that all financial statements included in consolidated financial statements should be prepared in conformity with U.S. generally accepted accounting principles. The Board concluded that consistency of accounting procedures and measurement processes between foreign and domestic operations is desirable in the consolidation of foreign and domestic financial statements. Therefore, foreign statements prepared for purposes of . . . consolidation . . . should be prepared in conformity with U.S. generally accepted accounting principles, and translation should not change the measurement bases used in those foreign statements." (Ibid., paragraph 82, pp. 38-39.)

Later the FASB stated "the Board believes that consideration of fundamental changes in generally accepted accounting principles relating to measurement bases of assets and liabilities is beyond this Statement's scope. The Board does not intend to use translation procedures to effect major changes in the accounting model presently in use." (Ibid., paragraph 110, p. 51.)

[8] The FASB stated "Since for the reasons given, the Board chose an objective of translation and a translation procedure that preserve the present accounting model, it rejected proposed Objective E." (Ibid., paragraph 111, p. 51.) Objective E is "To produce an exchange gain or loss that is compatible with the expected economic effect of a rate change on business activities conducted in a currency other than dollars." (Ibid., paragraph 79, p. 38.)

In addition, see the views of Mr. Mays in his (lone) dissenting opinion on *Statement No. 8* (ibid., pp. 16-18) and the comments of Donald Kirk (like Mays a member of the FASB) at the AEI-Treasury Conference on Exchange Rate Flexibility, April 20-22, 1976.

cost according to generally accepted accounting measures. And the FASB ruled that fixed assets are to be translated at historical exchange rates.

The temporal method also requires inventories to be translated at historical exchange rates (except in situations where market value—that is, current value in foreign currency translated at current exchange rates—is lower than cost), since inventories are evaluated at historical prices on the basis of generally accepted accounting measures (except in situations where market value is lower than cost). And the FASB ruled that inventories are to be translated in this manner.

For long-term liabilities denominated in a foreign currency, there does not appear to be a coincidence between the logic of the temporal method and the FASB's ruling. Since bonds (and other long-term debt) are typically valued in terms of the historical interest rate (not the current, or market, interest rate), the temporal method would suggest that they should be translated at the historical exchange rate. The FASB, however, ruled that they should be translated at the current rate of exchange.

In this particular ruling, the FASB's method of translation appears to be illogical in view of the temporal method that the board was allegedly using. It would appear that the FASB was faced with a dilemma. Either the board could adhere to its logic and rule in favor of an historical exchange rate, or it could rely on economic reality and rule in favor of a current exchange rate. The FASB, in effect, made the latter choice.

It is possible to adopt a slightly different way of viewing the FASB decision on long-term debt denominated in a foreign currency. The FASB may have viewed the monetary–nonmonetary breakdown as being the best one, but the methodology as being deficient. Hence it adopted the temporal method, which is the more logical method. However, faced with the problem of translating long-term debt, it in effect decided that the implications of generally accepted accounting rules could not be supported in this one case.[9]

---

[9] Some support for this view may be found in paragraph 124, *Statement No. 8*. In it, the FASB states, "The translation procedures to apply the temporal method are generally the same as those now used by many U.S. enterprises under the monetary-nonmonetary method. The results of the temporal method and the monetary-nonmonetary method now coincide because under present generally accepted accounting principles monetary assets and liabilities are usually measured at amounts that pertain to the balance sheet date, and nonmonetary assets and liabilities are usually measured at prices in effect when the assets or liabilities were acquired or incurred. The monetary-nonmonetary classification itself contains nothing to preserve the measurement bases . . . that are in the foreign statements. Rather, the coincidence of results between the monetary-nonmonetary method and the temporal method is due solely to the nature of

Digression on the Method of Evaluating Long-Term Debt. There has been some discussion to the effect that long-term debt is really not valued at historical cost; rather, that it is measured in terms of its present value, since it is carried at redemption value discounted by the historical interest rate. I do not find this argument convincing. The implicit or explicit use of an historical interest rate for discounting purposes indicates that the debt is being valued at its historical price. When one uses marginal analysis, it is clear that even one second before the debt is to be repaid, its current price and historical price are probably not the same.

In the long run, it is true that long-term debt outstanding will usually be paid off in full. But this consideration really misses the point. Indeed, I have advisedly used the words, "outstanding" and "usually." Some debt may be prepaid at prices different from the historical price. And some debt may never be repaid or may be done so at only a fraction of the amount due. Indeed, there is always the possibility that the price of long-term debt may go to zero.

The appropriate method of evaluating long-term debt is a complex issue. Certainly, one would not want to value such debt at its current price if the historical cost valuation of certain assets were to continue: to do so might serve to improve the balance sheet position of a firm that is in the process of going bankrupt. The complexity of the issue is due to the interrelationship of assets and liabilities on a balance sheet. If a company were going bankrupt, the value of the liabilities would be decreasing, but this would be occasioned by a decline in the value of the assets.

It would appear to be useful to have the movement towards bankruptcy discernible on a balance sheet. This may of course suggest the desirability of retaining the existing method of valuing long-term debt, but altering the method of valuing certain assets.

---

present generally accepted accounting principles—assets and liabilities are measured on bases that happen to coincide with their classifications as monetary and nonmonetary. . . . Since the temporal method retains the measurement bases of the foreign statements equally as well under all accounting methods based on exchange prices as it does under historical cost accounting, the Board believes that it is the more generally valid method for achieving the objective of translation. It provides a conceptual basis for the procedures that are now used to apply the monetary-nonmonetary method."

2

ECONOMIC ANALYSIS OF ACCOUNTING STANDARDS

As was mentioned earlier, with economic value accounting standards, accounting data and economic values would correspond, both ex post and ex ante. Let us assume that, despite the practical problems, we have these standards.

In an economic value accounting system, the accounting and economic exposure of an asset or liability would, by definition, be the same. Both would refer, *inter alia,* to the degree to which the current U.S. dollar value of these items change with changes in the exchange rate. Summing the exposure of all items on a balance sheet (with appropriate weights attached thereto) would give the accounting and economic exposure of the multinational corporation. Thus, the accounting exposure of a multinational would, by definition, be equal to its economic exposure.

Furthermore, and of greater significance, the firm's expected accounting exposure (EAE) would be equal to its expected economic exposure (EEE).[1] And since EEE would be the result of its optimal planned economic exposure (OPEE), EEE would be equal to OPEE (which is not necessarily zero, or neutral, exposure).[2] In this situation,

---

[1] The expected economic exposure of an asset or firm is a very complex issue. It involves not only a mean EEE but a probability distribution as well. This paper does not examine in detail the implications of the probability distribution attached to the EEE of an asset. Suffice it to say here that even if an asset and a liability had the same mean EEE, the respective probability distributions of the EEE might be very different. In this situation, a firm would not necessarily consider itself in a good hedged position even if it had equal values of foreign assets and liabilities with identical mean EEEs.

[2] The optimal planned economic exposure of a firm is not necessarily "zero." Hedging an exposure of an inventory or fixed assets, for example, entails costs. In addition the expected benefits from hedging differ among firms, because of differences in preferences and differences in degree of risk exposure. Typically, well-diversified firms will not benefit as much (if at all) from hedging as will

expected accounting exposure would thus be equal to optimal planned economic exposure.

This equality between EAE and OPEE is very important. It means, in effect, that the accounting treatment of a multinational's balance sheet will not have any effect on a multinational's behavior. The firm will behave the same, with or without the standards.

In examining the economic effects of the new accounting standards, we must keep in mind that we were moving from one second-best situation to another. The situation that had existed before the adoption of the new standards was certainly not satisfactory. Indeed, what had saved the prior situation from being chaotic was the efficiency of the market.

There are two ways of examining the effects of the new accounting standards: (1) to examine the effects of moving from an ideal state of accounting to the new standards or (2) to examine the effects of moving from the prior second-best situation to the new second-best situation. In a sense, the first way is much easier, because the effects are intuitively clear. The second way, however, is not as difficult as it may appear. If we assume that each firm, prior to the issuance of the new standards, had adopted the standard that had most closely approximated its economic situation, the second way is also clear. This assumption is in fact quite plausible. Indeed, it would have been in each firm's interest to have adopted a standard that brought the firm closest to the situation in which EAE equalled EEE (and OPEE). Of course, situations can change; but this does not alter the plausibility of the assumption, especially if the firm could have altered its standard.

Viewed in either of the two ways, the new accounting standards can be shown to have had some adverse effects. There is, however, a value in standardization. This value cannot be as easily quantified as some of the other factors that we are considering, but it does exist. Furthermore, in the uncertain world in which we are now living, the value and importance of standardization are likely to be much greater than they would be in a world of more certainty. Thus, although it can be shown that the new standards represent the worst of the second-best situations in terms of the distortions that they introduce, such an analysis is incomplete and the implications may be misleading. (This will be discussed in section 4.)

firms with subsidiaries in only one country. For these reasons, the optimal planned economic exposure of firms will typically differ, and all are likely to be different from zero. Cf. Robert Aliber, "The Short Guide to Corporate International Finances," unpublished monograph (mimeographed, 1975).

In the remainder of this chapter, I examine the economic effects of accounting standards with special reference to the new ones. Both types of methodology, discussed above, are employed. The first three sections of this chapter develop the microeconomic framework of analysis, while the final section brings together some macroeconomic as well as some microeconomic considerations.

1. Discrepancy between Accounting Data and Economic Values— Nature and Significance

The problem with the new accounting standards is the same as the problem with all the different standards that had been in existence: any equality between a firm's EAE and OPEE would be fortuitous. For reasons discussed above, the relationship between EAE and OPEE is likely to be worse under the new standards than it was before.

The burden of an unrealistic EAE typically consists of an increase in the expected volatility of paper earnings. As is explained in section 2 below, an EAE that is significantly different from OPEE is also likely to be significantly different from neutral exposure. As a result, large translation gains and losses will often occur with swings in exchange rates.[3]

If EAE is not equal to OPEE, the multinational may be adversely affected. Indeed, the existence of the inequality between EAE and OPEE is a necessary but not sufficient condition for the multinational to be adversely affected by reporting requirements. For almost all practical purposes, the discrepancy between EAE and OPEE would have an adverse effect on multinationals. This discrepancy typically will induce multinationals to make uneconomic alterations of their planned economic exposure—in effect, going from OPEE, their initial (and optimal) planned economic exposure, to a new (and suboptimal) planned economic exposure.[4]

For there to be no adverse effect, at least two conditions must hold: (1) the security market would have to be "perfectly efficient" in the semi-strong form, as a minimum [5] and (2) all corporate managers

---

[3] See, for example, Memorandum to Securities and Exchange Commission by Schlumberger Ltd., on paragraph 12 of FASB *Statement No. 8*, February 23, 1976.

[4] In this paper, OPEE will refer to the optimal planned economic exposure in a world in which accounting standards do not introduce discrepancies between reported data and economic values, unless indicated otherwise.

[5] As William Beaver has pointed out, three forms of market efficiency have been delineated: "(1) the weak form, which deals with efficiency—with respect to the past sequence of security prices (e.g., the random-walk hypothesis), (2) the semi-strong form, which concerns efficiency with respect to published information, and

would have to consider it optimal to behave as if perfectly efficient markets did exist. Let us examine each of these conditions.

Efficiency of Security Market. A large amount of empirical literature suggests that the market is quite efficient in going around accounting information to get at economic values.[6] Indeed, many of the studies suggest that the window dressing of balance sheets has little effect on the market's evaluation of securities, except for a possible short-run effect.[7] If this is true, then the "window undressing" of balance sheets by the new accounting standards should not have much of an adverse effect on the market's evaluation of debt and equities.

A word of caution, however, should be introduced here. If, let us say, the new accounting standards produce a greater volatility of reported earnings than existed under the previous standards, and if the credit rating companies react to this greater volatility by lowering the ratings of the companies involved, the market's efficiency might be impaired.

In this connection, it should be borne in mind that in the market, most investors are naïve. The efficiency of the market is attributable to a relatively few knowledgeable investors (mostly large investors) as well as to reporting requirements and financial technology that disseminate useful data to these investors.[8] If institutional investors were constrained (by prospectuses and agreements) from effective arbitrage among securities in different credit ratings, the concentration on reported earnings by credit rating agencies might reduce the efficiency of the market.

Behavior of Corporate Managers. A crucial issue is whether corporate managers alter their planned economic exposure if there is a discrepancy between OPEE and EAE. To simplify the matter, let us assume (this assumption is not essential) that the EAE will produce

---

(3) the strong form, which involves all information including inside information." See William Beaver, "What Should Be the FASB's Objectives?" *Journal of Accountancy*, vol. 136, no. 2 (August 1973), pp. 49-56.

[6] See, for example, Beaver, "What Should Be the FASB's Objectives?"; Henry Wallich and Mable Wallich, "Profits Aren't As Good As They Look," *Fortune*, vol. 89, no. 3 (March 1974); and references in Thomas R. Dyckman, David H. Downes, and Robert P. Magee, *Efficient Capital Markets and Accounting: A Critical Analysis* (Englewood Cliffs, N.J.: Prentice Hall, Inc., 1975), chapter 2.

[7] See Wallich and Wallich, "Profits Aren't As Good As They Look." The possible short-run effect of window dressing presumably is reduced or eliminated as the market learns what is happening.

[8] Cf. Beaver, "What Should Be the FASB's Objectives?" and Dyckman, Downes, and Magee, *Efficient Capital Markets and Accounting*, pp. 6-7.

a greater volatility of reported earnings than the EEE. Will this have an effect on corporate managers? Will corporate managers alter their planned economic exposure? The answers would appear to be in the affirmative. Let us see why.

Perhaps the markets are not as efficient as some academic research would have us believe. Indeed, even in the academic literature, there are a few papers which suggest that the market is not as efficient as is suggested by some of the studies cited earlier.[9]

What is probably more important, however, is that, irrespective of the actual degree of the market's efficiency, corporate managers may not believe that the market is efficient. Alternatively, they may believe that the issue is irrelevant. Or, they may be unaware of the issue, but act as if it were irrelevant. Or, they may think that the owners are not concerned about market efficiency. Or, they may not believe that the owners will read the footnotes that seek to distinguish accounting data and economic data.[10] Furthermore, even if owners do read the footnotes, they might not be able to distinguish accounting data and economic data.

For one or more of these reasons, corporate managers would act as if the market were inefficient. Furthermore, even if the managers believed that the market were efficient, they might act otherwise. For example, they might be induced by bonuses—which they typically receive on the basis of reported (paper) earnings—to act otherwise. Indeed, to the extent that they are risk averters, the bonuses (for paper performance) would be effective in altering their behavior. Also, if the shareholders or boards of directors were concerned only about

---

[9] See Dyckman, Downes, and Magee, *Efficient Capital Markets and Accounting*, chapter 3.

[10] Well, at least you read a footnote. But what percentage of U.S. stockholders will do as you just did?

In this connection, paragraph no. 32 of *Statement No. 8* specifies that "the aggregate exchange gain or loss included in determining net income for the period shall be disclosed in the financial statements or in a note thereto."

In addition, paragraph no. 33 states, "Effects of rate changes on reported results of operations, other than the effects included in the disclosure required by paragraph 32, shall, if practicable, be described and quantified. If quantified, the methods and the underlying assumptions used to determine the estimated effects shall be explained."

There is no discussion on the disclosure of future effects of rate changes. Such a disclosure is neither prohibited nor required. These future effects are of course important in affecting, *inter alia*, the present value of a firm's fixed assets. I expect very few firms will make such a disclosure. Furthermore, such disclosures would not likely alter the behavior of corporate managers, which is the crux of the problem. The only (apparent) benefit of the disclosures might be to make the existing market (which already appears to be efficient) a little more efficient.

paper earnings, the managers might be induced or forced (by the threat of removal) to act as if the market were not efficient.

Certainly, the financial press concentrates on the reporting of accounting data. This concentration may well serve to reinforce the concerns of shareholders and boards of directors about reported earnings.

Corporate managers could, of course, prepare two sets of books— an internal economic book for their boards of directors and an external accounting book required by the FASB. Undoubtedly, some firms will do this. But for this practice to enable corporate managers to be unaffected by accounting distortions, the managers and boards of directors would have to recognize the problems they face and be immune from criticism (and perhaps removal) by shareholders.

Many corporate directors are unable to comprehend their managers' new reports which are laced with footnotes and qualifications. In particular, they are unable to distinguish the froth from the economic earnings of subsidiaries. As a result, their ability to control the companies that they direct has been impaired by the new standards.

Empirical data on corporate behavior under the new accounting standards confirm the hypothesis that corporate managers are affected by the discrepancy between accounting and economic data.[11] One possible long-run constraint on the managers' ability to make suboptimal economic decisions for the firm is that the company may eventually become ripe for a takeover, because of the opportunity for the astute investor to receive an abnormally large return from redressing the nonoptimal decision making. This long-run possibility may induce corporate managers to launch a campaign designed to educate the firm's board of directors and stockholders. Of course, such a campaign would entail costs as well as benefits, and it thus may not eliminate the problem, even over an extended period of time.

The important points are, first, that there are a large number of reasons why corporate managers either believe that the market is inefficient (or, more precisely, less than perfectly efficient) or act as if they hold this belief. And, second, corporate managers do in fact behave as if the market were inefficient (or, more precisely, less than perfectly efficient). To state the two points differently (and more simply), corporate managers are affected by the discrepancy between accounting and economic data.

---

[11] Rita Rodriguez of Harvard University has collected a large body of evidence confirming the effects that accounting standards have had on managerial decision making in multinational firms. Also, see note 19 to this chapter.

2. Discrepancy between Accounting Data and Economic Values— The New Standards

As was indicated in section 1 above, the discrepancy between a firm's EAE and EEE (the latter resulting from OPEE) provides the basis of our understanding the adverse effects facing multinationals under the new accounting standards. This section examines the nature of this discrepancy by focusing on the controversial items on the firm's balance sheet.

In effect, the new standards treat long-term debt (as well as short-term debt) denominated in a foreign currency as being exposed to changes in exchange rates since such debt must be revalued in end-of-period reporting statements. The new standards treat inventories and fixed assets as being unexposed since such items are not to be revalued.

In some situations, this accounting treatment of exposure to exchange risk (the risk of changes in exchange rates) may be reasonably consistent with a firm's economic exposure. Indeed, that is undoubtedly why many firms had opted for the old monetary–nonmonetary standard.

In the case of long-term debt denominated in a foreign currency, there is no question that its value in U.S. dollars does change with every change in the exchange rate, and thus the accounting treatment and economic reality are consistent. It is true that if the expected changes in exchange rates are reflected in interest differentials, and if these expectations are borne out, then one could consider long-term debt as being unexposed to exchange risk. The degree, however, to which exchange rate expectations are borne out varies greatly as a result, *inter alia*, of differences in time horizons, differences in currencies, and differences in time periods.[12] For this reason, the accounting treatment of long-term debt denominated in a local currency appears to be correct.

For fixed assets and most inventories, the situation is much more complex.[13] It is often difficult to know the nature of the economic

---

[12] Cf. Robert Z. Aliber and Clyde T. Stickney, "Accounting Measures of Foreign Exchange Exposure: The Long and Short of It," *The Accounting Review*, vol. 50, no. 1 (January 1975). Aliber and Stickney present a lot of evidence indicating that over long periods, exchange rate expectations are borne out quite well. However, for the reasons suggested in the text, other considerations are also important in determining appropriate accounting treatment. Furthermore, even if the long-period consideration were the only one, the degree to which expectations are borne out in the future may differ from the degree to which they have been borne out in the past.

[13] Inventories whose rate of turnover is expected to be very high do not present a significant exposure problem.

exposure of these assets. In all likelihood, the expected economic exposure (EEE) of inventories and fixed assets is known best by the firm itself. In any case, the realized economic exposure (REE) is an important factor affecting the EEE. In examining the REE of non-monetary assets, we must take care to distinguish between the effects of exchange rate changes and those of other factors.

The following are among the factors that affect the degree of economic exposure of a firm's nonmonetary assets: (1) the degree to which the subsidiary's output is exported, (2) the degree to which the subsidiary employs imported factors of production, and (3) the degree of flexibility of the subsidiary's operation.[14]

To ascertain the EEE of a firm's fixed assets and inventories, it is necessary to consider both past experience and the expectation as to how likely such experience is to be continued. For example, a firm would not consider its fixed assets or inventories as being exposed under the following conditions: (1) the existence in the past of a perfect purchasing-power-parity relationship between a foreign currency and the U.S. dollar, (2) the existence in the past of a perfect correlation between the local currency price of the fixed assets and inventory and the general price index in the foreign country, and (3) an expectation by the firm that the first two conditions would hold in the future.[15]

Needless to say, neither of the first two assumptions may hold, especially in the short run. Furthermore, the degree to which the second assumption is approximated will vary from company to company. In addition, for a given company, the degree to which these assumptions are approximated will vary from one point in time to another; from one period to another (as, for example, from the 1950s to the 1970s); from a short-run time horizon to a long-run time horizon; from investment in one region to that in another (as, for example, from Latin America to Europe); from investment in one country to that in another (as, for example, from the United Kingdom to West Germany); from investment in one type of asset to another (as, for example, from fixed assets to inventory); and from investments of one nature to another (as, for example, from investment in assets made

---

[14] See Gunter Dufey, "Corporate Financial Policies and Floating Exchange Rates," an address presented at the meeting of the International Fiscal Association in Rome (Italy), on October 14, 1974. Published as Dufey, *Politica finanziaria di un'impresa in un contesto di oscillazioni del tasso di cambio* (Padua: Casa Editrice Dott. Antonio Milani, 1975).

[15] To the extent that the expectation in the third condition is not held with certainty, there would be an exposure cost of investing abroad. See note 1 to this chapter.

in the United States to those acquired locally).[16] Finally, even if the first two assumptions did hold, it does not follow that the third assumption would, especially in a rapidly changing world economy.

The important points are, first, that there are large differences in the REE of nonmonetary assets and, second, that such differences are likely to persist. Good illustrations of the differences in the REE of nonmonetary assets are contained in the FASB *Discussion Memorandum*.[17] In view of these points, the EEEs of such assets are also likely to be very different. No accounting system short of one based on current value could accommodate these different EEEs.

Furthermore, if one considers (1) the probable wide differences between firms in the EEE of their nonmonetary assets, (2) the differences between firms in the location of their foreign investments, (3) the differences between firms in the expected variability of exchange rates, (4) the differences between firms in the degree of their concern about economic exposure, and (5) the probable wide differences in hedging costs between firms (a point discussed in a different context in the next section), it is not difficult to recognize the wide differences that are likely to exist in the OPEE of different firms. And no accounting system short of one based on current value could accommodate these different OPEEs.

Indeed, it would be fortuitous for the EAE for any given nonmonetary asset to be equal to its EEE, and it would be fortuitous for the EAE of any given firm to be equal to its EEE (and OPEE). The discrepancy between the EAE and the EEE (and OPEE) of a firm induces uneconomic adjustments that are discussed in the next section.

Furthermore, the issuance of *Statement No. 8* in all probability exacerbated the discrepancies between EAE and OPEE, as indicated earlier. Indeed, there may in fact have been good reasons why many foreign subsidiaries issued long-term debt denominated in the local currency to finance fixed asset investments abroad or why many foreign subsidiaries issued short-term debt denominated in the local currency to purchase inventories.

In all likelihood, the foreign subsidiaries that had a rough equivalence between short-term debt denominated in the local currency and inventories or between long-term debt denominated in the local cur-

---

[16] Cf. Aliber and Stickney, "Accounting Measures of Foreign Exchange Exposure." Aliber and Stickney present evidence suggesting that purchasing power parity holds quite well in the long run. For individual assets, however, it is not likely to hold nearly as well in the long run.

[17] Financial Accounting Standards Board, *Discussion Memorandum: An Analysis of Issues Related to Accounting for Foreign Currency Translation* (Stamford, Connecticut: FASB, 1975).

rency and fixed assets would not have been employing the monetary–nonmonetary standards prior to the issuance of *Statement No. 8*. For such firms, the new standards are likely to change their EAE from an exposure position relatively close to zero to one characterized by a large net short position.

Empirically, *Statement No. 8* increases the net short position of some firms' EAE. Indeed, since the new accounting standards translate inventories at historical exchange rates, whereas many firms had been using current exchange rates for such translation, the new ruling will decrease the volume of assets to be revalued at current exchange rates, thereby increasing the net short position of such firms. And since the new accounting standards translate long-term foreign currency debt at current exchange rates, whereas some firms had been using historical exchange rates for such translation, the new ruling will increase the volume of liabilities to be revalued at current exchange rates, thereby also increasing the net short position of such firms.

There has been some discussion to the effect that reported earnings of some firms may be rendered more stable by the issuance of *Statement No. 8*. The implication is that for some firms the new EAE might be closer to zero than the old EAE. There has also been some discussion to the effect that the greater stability in reported earnings will have beneficial effects, perhaps offsetting or at least mitigating the adverse effects of the alternative situation.

Let us assume, as is plausible, that prior to the issuance of *Statement No. 8*, a firm's decision on its accounting standards was determined on the basis of the proximity of EAE to OPEE. If firms' OPEEs were randomly distributed around zero within a fairly small range (a not unlikely situation under floating rates), and if the increase in the net short position of EAE were relatively large, it would be virtually impossible to have a greater stability of reported earnings under *Statement No. 8*. If, however, some firms had a positive OPEE (and surely many had), and if the shift in EAE is not too large (and probably for a few firms, this will be the case), then the situation envisaged may in fact occur for a few firms.

But even for the few firms that might secure greater stability of reported earnings under the new standards, it is not clear that there would be any benefits from this greater stability. Indeed, the firms involved may be induced by the altered position of their EAE to change their planned economic exposure. If this happens, the firm will be moving away from its OPEE, and this will have all the adverse consequences that nonoptimal decision making brings forth. (This point will be discussed in the next section.)

There has also been some discussion to the effect that in the long run, after all assets have turned over, or have been disposed of, the accumulated total earnings of the company will be the same, whether on an accounting or economic basis, if we abstract from tax considerations.[18] The important point, however, is that the alteration in the expected time path of earnings may have adverse (perhaps highly adverse) effects on some companies. In particular, to the extent that the discrepancy between the expected time profile of reported earnings and the expected time profile of economic earnings induces corporate managers to alter their company's planned economic exposure away from its OPEE, the company will be adversely affected.

3. Adjustment Costs Induced by Discrepancy between Accounting Data and Economic Values

Corporate managers may be concerned about the nature of the new EAE, which may differ significantly from OPEE and "zero" exposure. In all likelihood, as was suggested in the previous section, the new EAE will be further from zero than the old EAE, and will therefore entail a greater expected variability of reported earnings.

As was indicated earlier (section 1 of this chapter), corporate managers are affected by the discrepancy between accounting and economic data. They may react to the new time profile of expected reported earnings by altering their accounting exposure. One or more of several actions may be taken to reduce the net short EAE; these actions may be described as "hedges." In the usual terminology, hedges refer to financial actions taken to mitigate or eliminate net real (or commercial) open positions so as to reduce economic uncertainty; in the present context, the word "hedges" has, paradoxically, the broader connotation of real as well as financial actions taken to reduce "accounting uncertainty."

The hedging adjustments made by firms, however, affect not only EAE but also EEE. In particular, the net short EAE will be reduced, but the net long EEE will be enhanced. Indeed, the actions taken will typically entail a movement away from a firm's OPEE, its optimal decision-making strategy.

Empirical research, as pointed out earlier, has in fact shown that the new accounting methods of translating balance sheet items have affected corporate decision making. Conversations with and articles

---

[18] The IRS formulates its own rules on corporate earnings and these may or may not be the same as accounting standards. The accounting standards may of course influence the IRS rulings, and perhaps vice versa.

by bankers, security analysts, and economists readily confirm the existence of these effects.[19] The methods and magnitude of hedging adjustments induced by *Statement No. 8* will be a function of a number of variables—both demand and supply.

The demand (in an economic sense) for hedging adjustments by corporate managers will be a function, *inter alia*, of the following: the magnitude of shift in a firm's EAE occasioned by the new standards, the degree to which the company's managers ignore the market efficiency argument (which itself is a function of a number of variables described earlier), and the expected variability of the relevant exchange rate(s).

On the supply side, the relevant variable is the cost of hedging. Two types of costs must be distinguished. One type is the direct costs—the transaction costs and other costs directly associated with the hedging adjustments that are induced by the shift in EAE. The second type is the indirect costs—the costs to the firm of having its planned economic exposure different from its OPEE.

The cost of hedging—direct and indirect—is a function of the method(s) used as well as the relevant magnitude(s). Presumably a firm will select the least-cost method(s). Different methods will be employed by different companies because of differences in firms' characteristics (including skills) as well as differences in situations (actual and perceived).

In this connection, it should be noted that income statements and balance sheet statements are interrelated, as are (one may assume) the types of hedging that are covered by the respective statements. This interrelationship would appear to be an interesting area for study, but has not, so far as I am aware, received any attention.

There are two general ways of hedging that should be distinguished: financial and real. Financial hedging consists largely of two methods: borrowing (or lending) in foreign currencies and the use of forward contracts. For the financial adjustments, the direct costs are likely to be much less than the indirect costs.

The real hedge. Real hedging (as opposed to financial) may take the form of a diversification of direct investment abroad or perhaps of a reduction or elimination of the foreign subsidiary's operation. In the case of real adjustments, the indirect costs may be expected to

---

[19] See, for example, Dufey, "Corporate Financial Policies and Floating Exchange Rates," and the references contained therein, and Alan Teck, "International Business under Floating Rates" (paper presented at the AEI—Treasury Conference on Exchange Rate Flexibility, Washington, D.C., April 20-22, 1976). Also, see note 11 to this chapter.

be negative, but by definition will be less in absolute amount than the direct costs.

The accounting-induced movement of a firm away from its OPEE will have adverse effects. In particular, it will directly generate a lower and/or more variable real rate of return. In addition, if the security market is very efficient, additional adverse effects will occur. A reduced price-earnings ratio and higher borrowing costs will reflect a firm's worsened real situation. In turn, the security market, through the alteration in the cost of capital, will have an adverse repercussive effect on the firm.

These adverse economic effects resulting from the accounting-induced adjustments made by firms in their planned economic exposure help to constrain them in the degree to which they react to their accounting distortion. Needless to say, firms will differ in the degree of importance that they attach to an accounting distortion, as well as in the economic costs of adjusting thereto. For these reasons, *inter alia*, firms are likely to differ in their reactions to a given accounting distortion. Furthermore, many firms are likely to alter their reactions over time, if for no other reason than the fact that corporate managers are likely to vacillate in the relative importance that they attach to accounting and economic exposure. This vacillation may be due to changes in the managers' subjective preferences. More likely it will be due to changes in their environment—as, for example, the degree of competition facing the firm, the concerns of shareholders and the corporations' directors, and the threat of bankruptcy.

This discussion suggests an interesting area for study—namely, the characteristics of a company (including skills) that are likely to lead to different methods and amounts of ("hedging") adjustments to the new accounting standards. Let us take real adjustments first. Several considerations bear on whether a firm is likely to diversify its foreign investment. One important consideration might be the degree of co-variation between the relevant currencies involved. Another consideration might be the capital intensity of the operation. Still another consideration might be marketing and purchasing factors, which bring us into a whole range of "geo-economic" issues.

In addition, it would be interesting to examine the characteristics of companies that reduce the scope of their foreign operations. One consideration might be the initial limited scope of the operations abroad. A second consideration might be the expected variability of the currency in question. A third consideration might be the standards employed prior to *Statement No. 8*.

In considering financial adjustments, we could also examine the characteristics of companies that adjust in different ways. In addition, we could try to ascertain why some types of adjustments are used extensively, while others are used relatively little.

Too little time has elapsed since *Statement No. 8* took effect to make more than a few tentative remarks on the adjustment methods being adopted by multinationals. The use of forward currency contracts appears to be increasing. One possible reason is that forward contracts may be supplanting short-term debt as a hedge against inventories where specific commitments of inventory sales have been made: *Statement No. 8* ruled that forward contracts specified by a firm as a commitment against future inventory sales would not be revalued at current exchange rates in end-of-period reporting statements.[20] In addition, forward contracts are now being used in ways no one had ever foreseen (a point to be discussed shortly).

Institutional factors, however, may to some extent be restricting the use of forward contracts as a hedging adjustment. In particular, tax laws may be a factor limiting the use of these contracts. This is a very complex and technical issue. It would appear that most gains on forward contracts are taxed as ordinary income, and that therefore, to secure an expected full offset of capital losses, transactions in the forward market may have to be twice as large as those they are designed to offset.[21] This tax consideration may make the indirect cost of adjustment through forward contracts relatively large.

The accounting hedge. A banker recently told me that some "weird things" were happening in the foreign exchange market. Some companies were, in effect, selling forward contracts in a given currency with a given maturity to themselves. The banker did not know why they were doing it and did not want to inquire.

The following rationale for this phenomenon should therefore be regarded cautiously. It does, however, appear to be plausible. Let us suppose that because of the new accounting standards, the net short position of a firm's EAE is increased. (This is the direction in which the standards would be pushing some firms, as was explained earlier.) Yet the composition of the firm's balance sheet will have been determined earlier on the basis of the EEE of its nonmonetary assets, the original EAE, and the demand and supply of adjustment hedges.

---

[20] Financial Accounting Standards Board, *Statement No. 8,* paragraphs 22-27. Many inventories, however, are held for general rather than specific customers. For these inventories, the use of forward contracts would be less effective than it would be for inventories held for specific commitments.

[21] See Aliber, "The Short Guide to Corporate International Finances."

The increase in the net short EAE is regarded as a cost by the firm, because of the distortion in the expected time path of earnings (and the likely increase in the expected variability of reported earnings). The firm would like to shift the EAE towards the original EAE. Ordinarily, one might expect a hedging adjustment—real or financial—that would move the new EAE towards the old EAE, but that would also alter the planned economic exposure (and EEE), leading to some adverse consequences for the firm, described earlier. It is these adverse effects that typically preclude a full adjustment by the firm to the original EAE, as was indicated earlier.

Under certain conditions, however, there may be a hedging adjustment mechanism through the forward market by which a firm may alter its expected accounting exposure without altering its planned and expected economic exposure. This might enable a firm to make a full adjustment in its accounting exposure, because the cost of adjustment is so low.

Let us see how this adjustment may be made. The hedging is carried out by a unique "straddle"—the simultaneous purchase and sale of a forward contract in the same foreign currency and for the same term to maturity. Two separate transactions are made between a company and a bank. The simultaneity of the transactions eliminates the search cost element in the bid-asked spread. Thus, the transactions can be effected for a nominal fee.

The long position of the "accounting straddle" (not a straddle in the usual sense of the term) is designed to serve as a hedge against the accounting short exposure. The short position of the "straddle" is specified by the firm as a commitment against a future inventory sale. In this situation, the long position of the "accounting straddle" would be revalued at the current exchange rate, thereby offsetting the revaluation of the accounting short exposure. The short position of the "straddle," since it was specified by the firm as a commitment against future inventory sales, would—by the rulings of *Statement No. 8*—not be revalued at current exchange rates in end-of-period reporting statements.

This adjustment—the "accounting hedge"—would appear to be advantageous for many firms, since there would be no indirect costs and only nominal direct costs. It is also probably the clearest example of the uneconomic adjustments that are being made by firms in response to *Statement No. 8*. Tax considerations as well as the requirement in *Statement No. 8* on the commitment against future inventory sales may of course limit the extent to which the accounting hedge may be used.

One final point on the accounting hedge is worth mentioning. This adjustment technique, although it appears to have the smallest adverse effect on the firm, may well have the largest impact on the FASB. Because the accounting hedge so clearly entails a pure and unadulterated waste of scarce resources, I venture the guess that either the FASB will rule against its use (which will make me regret that I discussed it) or it will help to expedite the process via which the new standards become old ones.

4. Economic Effects of New Accounting Standards

The new accounting standards (as is suggested by the previous discussion) are likely to have a wide array of effects. In particular, the volume of investment is likely to be curtailed and the allocation of resources for a given volume of investment is likely to be distorted. These effects result from the adjustment costs incurred by firms in reaction to *Statement No. 8*.

In the analysis so far, I have abstracted from the effects of *Statement No. 8* in bringing uniformity of treatment to the translation process. It is my view that the change in the translation process from one involving the simultaneous existence of numerous standards to the present uniformity of treatment will have some beneficial effects in addition to the adverse effects discussed above.

The value of standardization lies in the confidence that it transmits to and instills in the investment community. In particular, as a result of the standardization, social critics may become less concerned than in the past about alleged speculative activities carried out by multinationals and therefore may put less pressure on the government to control or regulate the multinationals. (Unfortunately, however, this beneficial effect on confidence may be offset to some extent by the accounting-induced increase in the volume of multinationals' speculation, and the concerns generated thereby. This point will be discussed in Chapter 3.)

The enhanced confidence may have a favorable direct effect on the market for the securities of multinationals. More importantly, perhaps, it may enable companies to have new flexibility in adjusting to economic exposure and to accounting distortions as well as to be less concerned about possible new governmental regulations and controls (a point discussed in Chapter 3).

For these reasons, I believe that the multinationals that had been using the old monetary–nonmonetary standard may be favorably affected by *Statement No. 8* and that the other multinationals that had been using alternative standards may not be as adversely affected as the earlier analysis suggested. The beneficial effects of standardization should not be ignored. Indeed, in the uncertain world in which we now live, the value and importance of standardization are likely to be greater than they would be in a world with more certainty.

On the firms that are adversely affected by the new accounting standards, the impact will not fall evenly. For example, small and thinly capitalized multinationals will be hurt relatively more than their larger and better capitalized associates. In addition, companies with a large investment in a single country will be affected more than companies that are effectively diversified. And companies with a subsidiary in a country with highly variable exchange rates may be affected more than companies with a subsidiary in countries with a stable economic climate.

There may be a difference between the effect of *Statement No. 8* on existing multinationals and its effect on similar multinationals formed after January 1, 1976. The existing multinationals that had not opted for the monetary–nonmonetary standards will have to adjust to the new standards from a position already outstanding (including, perhaps, long-term debt denominated in a foreign currency that cannot be prepaid). It may be much easier for new firms of a similar nature to adapt to the new standards.

In addition, *Statement No. 8* is likely to encourage the development of multinationals whose economic exposure is reasonably consistent with the accounting exposure of the new standards, and it is likely to discourage the development of multinationals whose economic exposure is very different from the accounting exposure formulated by the new standards. For all multinationals, the new standards are likely to lead to greater centralization than now exists in the planning and control of "exposure."

For corporate managers and firms that had established hedging positions on the basis of alternative standards, the new standards may have an equity as well as an efficiency effect. Corporate managers and firms that were pursuing prudent policies may now appear to be daring, and vice versa. In addition, individual investors may find themselves buying something different from what they think they are buying. An individual may think he is buying a blue chip when he is in effect buying a real lemon. The individual who is buying a real lemon will not, however, be paying an inflated price for it: the market will have priced the securities correctly from the viewpoint of economic earnings. Thus, instead of purchasing a blue chip at a bargain price, which is what the individual thinks he is doing, he will be buying a real lemon at its appropriate price.

There may be a short-run effect on the volume of transactions, as individual investors reshuffle their portfolios. Institutional investors may well increase their holdings of apparent lemons. And the new portfolios may well be more risky (or less risky) than the investors realize.

The new standards may induce the adversely affected multinationals to seek additional government intervention in exchange markets so as to secure greater stability in exchange rates. The effects of government intervention on the stability of a market is a complex issue. The idea of smoothing out changes in exchange rates induced by fundamental factors appears to be an attempt to retain the Bretton Woods principle of distinguishing between fundamental and nonfundamental factors affecting exchange rates. This distinction, however, is beset by numerous problems.[22] Indeed, the problems are such

---

[22] For example, it is difficult to determine ex ante what is and what is not a cycle-induced change in exchange rates. In part, the difficulty is attributable to the problem of ascertaining the phase of a business cycle that an economy is in. It is also attributable to the problem of predicting business cycles. Factors contributing to the prediction problem include the unpredictable nature of governmental macroeconomic policies, the difficulty of predicting business cycles in one country in relation to those in other countries, and the two-way causation between business cycles and exchange rates.

Even ex post, the effect of business cycles on exchange rates is a complex issue. Two principal cyclical effects must be distinguished. The traditional theoretical effect is the cycle's impact on trade flows: a decline in business activity will improve the balance of trade and thereby enhance the international value of the dollar. This traditional effect may, however, be swamped by the cycle-induced effect on expectations: a decline in business activity (or perhaps an acceleration in the rate of decline) may reduce investors' expectations of the real rate of growth of the U.S. economy, thereby decreasing net capital inflows to the United States, and thereby reducing the international value of the dollar.

The problem of ascertaining the effects of these two factors is greatly complicated by the existence of numerous other factors which may affect the exchange rate. In addition, although GNP is by definition the key element in a business cycle, there are other elements, such as interest rates and prices, that have an impact on exchange rates. And the cycles in the different elements of a business cycle have different and varying periodicities. For this reason, the problem of ascertaining the cycle's impact on exchange rates is greatly complicated.

If we assume that the effects of business cycles on exchange rates are clear, the crucial issue is whether speculators would smooth out the cycle-induced changes. This issue does not appear to have been resolved at the present time.

(This material was presented in my "Discussion" at the Treasury workshop on Technical Studies on Economic Interdependence and Exchange Rate Flexibility, February 26-27, 1976. I initially prepared the material as a memorandum at the Treasury Department, February 12, 1976.)

that government intervention at times (perhaps often) may itself become a new source of instability.

The new standards will affect the allocation of resources, both for the United States and for the world as a whole, as real resources are switched among multinationals as well as between multinationals and domestic firms. They will also affect financial markets, including the international currency markets, as was suggested in the preceding section. Indeed, many foreign exchange dealers have commented on the heavy volume of activity in the first week of January, an apparent indication of the effects of the new accounting standards (which took effect on January 1, 1976). Finally, the new standards will affect the economic exposure of many firms under floating rates and will create a bias against floating rates. Chapter 3 discusses these effects and their policy implications.

Several research areas would appear to be fruitful for testing the implications of points made in this chapter. They are discussed in the Appendix.

3

INTERNATIONAL FINANCE AND THE NEW ACCOUNTING STANDARDS

The first three sections of this chapter examine the implications of fixed (adjustable peg) and floating rate systems for uncertainty facing multinationals and for their behavior. In these sections, economic value accounting is assumed to exist.

In the first three sections, two basic questions are considered: what is the difference in the nature of uncertainty facing multinationals under fixed and floating rates? and how are firms able to cope with this uncertainty (that is, what is the cost of hedging) under the two exchange rate systems? Section 1 analyzes the cost of exposure and the cost of hedging, section 2 discusses the differences in the nature of hedging under fixed and floating rates, and section 3 examines uncertainty (initial and residual) under fixed and floating rates. Floating rates are shown to have a comparative advantage in reducing distant-term uncertainty, and fixed rates to have a comparative advantage in reducing near-term uncertainty (although floating rates may well have an absolute advantage in reducing both).

Section 4 discusses problems for multinationals and floating rates that were created by the new accounting standards. Section 5 examines some policy implications of these problems.

1. Cost of Exposure and Cost of Hedging

The benefits of hedging result from reductions in the cost of exposure. Thus, it is important to consider the meaning of the "cost of exposure."

The cost of exposure, for a given degree of expected exposure (of, let us say, nonmonetary assets), defined earlier, is a function of the expected level and variability of exchange rates. The cost of exposure

31

will typically differ both among firms and for a given firm over time, as a result of differences in the expected level and variability of exchange rates as well as of differences in risk aversion. To simplify the following discussion, we can assume—unless stated otherwise—that expectations are such that the expected future spot rate is equal to the current spot rate. This will enable us to examine more clearly the effects of uncertainty about future rates.

The cost of hedging depends of course on the way the hedging is carried out. As was mentioned earlier, hedging (and especially "hedging") can take a number of different forms. Presumably, firms use the least-cost method or combination of methods. To simplify the analysis, we will here consider—unless stated otherwise—hedging only through the forward market. This simplification should not affect the conclusions of the analysis.

In the forward market, the cost of hedging consists of transaction costs, which are a function, *inter alia*, of the bid-asked spread; and the difference between the forward (or future) rate on a foreign currency existing at a given point in time and the expected future spot rate (realized), which we will call the "futures discounts" or "futures premiums." (Whether it is a discount or premium depends on which side of the coin or currency we are looking at.) The futures discounts (premiums) are not the same things as the so-called "forward discounts"—the relationship between the current spot and current forward rate—that have often been used incorrectly as a measure of hedging cost. The futures discounts (premiums) are typically determined by the demand for contracts by hedgers (as a result of their cost of exposure) and the supply of contracts by speculators. (This will be discussed beginning on p. 34).

The cost of hedging, like the cost of exposure, will typically differ both among firms and for a given firm over time. Differences may exist in transaction costs and in the expected future spot rates, for a given forward rate. In addition, firms may differ in the degree of confidence with which they hold their expectations.

The uncertainty about the expected future spot rates is an important factor affecting the futures premiums as well as the transaction costs. The futures premiums and bid-asked spreads may be affected by other elements: expected voluntary and involuntary default and expected political risk.[1] Whether the cost of these elements is in-

---

[1] It has frequently been argued that political risk should be insured or guaranteed by the government, since commercial insurance is inherently incapable of dealing with it. See, for example, Marina Whitman, *Government Risk-Sharing in Foreign Investment* (Princeton: Princeton University Press, 1965), pp. 60-61. This argument, however, cannot be supported. On this point, see Joseph M. Burns,

cluded in the futures premium or bid-asked spread depends on whether there is an intermediary, such as a bank, in the transactions. The uncertainty about whether there is an intermediary is in fact why the futures premium was defined as the difference between the current forward (or future) rate and the expected future spot rate ("realized").

The existence of an intermediary is one factor that distinguishes a forward market from a futures market. In the forward market, a commercial bank plays an important intermediary role (over and above the transaction role) in the sense that it in effect serves to objectify some of the cost of hedging, by incorporating default risk and political risk in the bid-asked spread. The forward market may be viewed as a special type of futures market.

The futures premium and the transaction costs—which compose the "futures gap" (or wedge of finance costs between the hedger and speculator)—will differ both between currencies and among different forward maturities of a given currency.[2] In fact, for some currencies, forward contracts do not exist at all. For currencies where they do exist, they are limited to short and intermediate maturities. A similar situation exists with respect to commodities.

The absence of distant-term futures contracts means that investors are unable to hedge their net open positions in an effective way. As a result, multinational investment in new plant and equipment will be lower than it would otherwise be. In addition, the producers of industrial raw materials will be unable to hedge their investments effectively. As a result, future output will be lower than it would otherwise be, with adverse effects for both developed and developing countries.

"Alleged Market Failures in Financing U.S. Exports," in *Nuclear Proliferation: Future Foreign Policy Implications*, Hearings before the Subcommittee on International Security and Scientific Affairs of the House Committee on International Relations (Washington, D.C.: U.S. Government Printing Office, 1975), pp. 364-89, esp. pp. 386-88.

[2] The counterpart of the "futures gap" (in the forward markets) is the "spot gap" (in the loanable funds market). This latter gap consists of the cost of illiquidity and the cost of real uncertainty. These costs are reduced, *inter alia*, by financial intermediaries. For an examination of the spot gap, or "gap," see Joseph M. Burns, "The Saving-Investment Process in a Theory of Finance" (unpublished Ph.D. dissertation, University of Chicago, 1967) and "On the Effects of Financial Innovations," *Quarterly Review of Economics and Business*, vol. 11, no. 2 (Summer 1971).

For a discussion of international factors affecting the size of the spot gap, see Joseph M. Burns, "Comments" (on international financial intermediation), in Machlup, Salant, and Tarshis, eds., *International Mobility and Movement of Capital* (New York: Columbia University Press for National Bureau of Economic Research, 1972), pp. 676-81.

The absence of many types of forward contracts should not be viewed as a deficiency of financial adjustments in general or of forward markets in particular. Market forces determine both the types of forward contracts that do emerge and their maturity limits. The interrelationship of financial markets and the real sector is important but it has not, in my view, been sufficiently explored.[3] One possible reason is that economists do not ask often enough the question "Why do certain things happen, while other things do not happen?" A second possible reason is that economists usually lack the second-by-second knowledge of the market that is often crucial to a full understanding of why certain things happen while others do not.

As is explained below, it is in fact no surprise that distant-term forward (or futures) contracts have not appeared either in the industrial raw materials or in foreign currencies. It is also no surprise that near-term futures contracts have not developed for certain currencies. The analysis in the text, although of general applicability, focuses on currency futures.[4]

With hedging demand largely or entirely on one side of the market, a viable forward (futures) market would need to have speculators on the opposite side of the market willing to assume positions at prices acceptable to the hedgers. Speculators, however, will not take an open position unless they can receive what they consider to be sufficient compensation for their service.

Speculators are, in effect, providing insurance to hedgers—through the assumption of the risk of price volatility—and they must receive sufficient compensation to be willing to provide this service. As Keynes has pointed out, the cost of providing this insurance is typically "very high, much higher than is charged for any other form of insurance, though perhaps it is inevitable that a risk which only averages out over units spread *through time* should be less easy to insure than one which averages out over units which are nearly simultaneous—for we have to wait too long for the actuarial result."[5]

Thus, the crucial issue regarding the viability of forward (or future) currency contracts has been the strength of the demand by

[3] See, however, Frederick Lavington, *The English Capital Market* (London: Methuen and Co., Ltd., 1921); John G. Gurley and E. S. Shaw, *Money in a Theory of Finance* (Washington: The Brookings Institution, 1960); and Burns, "The Saving-Investment Process in a Theory of Finance."

[4] Some special factors applying to commodity futures are discussed by Joseph M. Burns, "Futures Contracts, Resource Allocation, and Governmental Policy" (mimeographed, June 30, 1975). Cf. J. R. Hicks, *Value and Capital* (Oxford: The Clarendon Press 1939), chapter 10.

[5] J. M. Keynes, "Some Aspects of Commodity Markets," *The Manchester Guardian*, March 29, 1923, emphasis in original.

hedgers (usually U.S. investors) for forward contracts compared with the willingness of speculators to assume the risk of an open position. For certain currencies, the strength of the hedgers' demand has simply not been sufficient to induce speculators to enter the market. And for distant maturities of all forward currency contracts, a similar situation exists. In both of these situations, the maximum price that hedgers have been willing to pay for insurance (the demand price) has been less than the minimum price that speculators have been willing to charge for providing this service (the supply price).

Speculators have shown a preference for assuming positions on near-term forward contracts of currencies of major industrial countries. For these contracts, the speculators have had a relatively low supply price—this being the difference between the average price expected by speculators on the realization of the contract and the price at which they are willing to assume a position.

The speculators' preference for the currencies of the developed countries is attributable, in part, to the greater hedging interest in the forward contracts of such currencies. Indeed, the literature on commodities futures has well-documented evidence that hedging interest is a necessary condition for the inception of a futures contract.[6] The reason for this is straightforward: speculators cannot make money unless there are others who are willing to lose money. And the more people (hedgers) there are who are willing to lose money, and the greater the urgency with which they wish to lose it, the greater the prospective returns become, *ceteris paribus*.

Speculators' preference for near-term (as opposed to distant-term) forward currency contracts is attributable, *inter alia*, to their greater ability to predict near-term prices as well as the greater volatility of such prices. The longer the time horizon, the more difficult predictions of future prices become. The principal reason for

---

[6] See Roger W. Gray and David J. S. Rutledge, "The Economics of Commodity Futures Markets: A Survey," *Review of Marketing and Agricultural Economics*, vol. 39, no. 4 (December 1971), pp. 57-108, esp. pp. 58-63. Gray and Rutledge state, "It is first of all clear that futures trading grew out of the merchandising trade already in existence." [References are here made to H. S. Irwin, *Evolution of Futures Trading* (Madison, Wisconsin: Mimir Publishers, Inc., 1954); C. H. Taylor, *History of the Board of Trade of the City of Chicago* (Chicago: Robert O. Law Co., 1917); and H. Working, "Economic Functions of Futures Markets," in H. Bakken, ed., *Futures Trading in Livestock—Origins and Concepts* (Madison, Wisconsin: Mimir Publishers, Inc., 1970)]. Gray and Rutledge continue, "Merchants, dealers, processors, etc., the regular tradespeople, organized the markets to better facilitate the trading they were already engaged in. An alternative possibility—that they might have been organized by persons outside the trade who were desirous of speculating in price movements—finds no historical support" (p. 58).

this is that distant spot prices depend on government policies that have not yet been determined and on unforeseen structural changes in the private sector.

On the basis of past experience, government policy actions cannot be easily predicted. Indeed, the shifts of government policies in the industrial countries over the past decade have served to increase distant-term uncertainty. In a recent paper, Benjamin Klein has presented evidence suggesting "that over the last decade the public has recognized that a major institutional monetary change has occurred and that perceived long-term price uncertainty has increased relative to short-term uncertainty. The long-term movement of the monetary framework away from a gold exchange commodity standard accelerated over the postwar period and has finally culminated in an irredeemable pure fiduciary standard."[7]

With regard to the risk of distant-term uncertainty, it would appear to be useful to distinguish the risk of uncertainty about future government macro policy, or "macro risk," from the risk of uncertainty about future relative prices, or "micro risk." The longer the time period, the greater the macro risk is likely to become in relation to micro risk.

Speculators cannot provide insurance very easily against the distant-term macro risk. Indeed, such macro risk has a very high cost of which speculators are well aware. By comparison, the distant-term micro risk has a relatively low cost.

An indexed forward contract may well increase speculative interest in the distant-term forward markets. This would reduce distant-term risk by reducing the high cost component (macro risk).

The Gold Clause Joint Resolution of June 5, 1933, and subsequent court decisions, however, have cast some doubt on the enforceability of indexed contracts,[8] thereby perhaps constraining the development of such a market. In the current economic environment, there does not appear to be any benefit to retention of the gold clause. Indeed, given the U.S. government's stated objective of a complete end to the monetary role of gold (that is, to treat gold in a manner similar to that in which other commodities are treated), congressional repeal of the gold clause would seem to be desirable.

---

[7] Klein, "Our New Monetary Standard: The Measurement and Effects of Price Uncertainty, 1880-1973," p. 482.

[8] Under the Gold Clause Joint Resolution of June 5, 1933, contractual provisions for the payment in gold coin were ruled unenforceable. A subsequent decision by the U.S. Supreme Court (1939) extended the gold clause to multiple currencies. A recent decision by the Supreme Court of Tennessee (October 1975) extended the gold clause to a promissory note with an indexation of principal.

Price volatility is conducive to speculation because it opens up the possibility of high rates of return for a given capital position. In his treatise, *Value and Capital*, J. R. Hicks observed that short-term interest rates fluctuate more than long-term interest rates. Long-term rates are, in effect, an average of expected short-term rates, abstracting from the cost of illiquidity (which is a function of real investors' preference for illiquidity, lenders' risk of being illiquid, lenders' attitude towards this risk, and the efficiency of speculation).[9] For futures prices, a similar situation exists. Near-term futures prices tend to fluctuate more than would those of the distant maturities. The prices of distant maturities would be, in effect, an average of expected short-term prices, abstracting from the cost of insurance (which is a function of hedgers' preference for long-term risk reduction, and speculators' willingness to bear this risk).[10]

As was noted earlier, the prices of distant-term currency contracts are difficult to predict. In fact, it would appear to be more difficult to predict such prices than it is to predict a long-term interest rate: the long-term interest rate is affected primarily by expectations about conditions in only one country, whereas the price of distant-term currency contracts is affected primarily by expectations about conditions in two countries.

For this reason, the risk premiums embedded in forward short-term currency rates should be greater than those embedded in forward short-term interest rates. As a result, the average "backwardation" of distant-term currency futures (where hedging occurs primarily on one side of the market) should typically be greater than the risk premiums embedded in long-term interest rates. For this reason, we should not expect the forward maturities of currency contracts to be extended as far as the term to maturity of loan contracts. In addition, we should not expect firms to hedge through the forward market if it is possible

---

[9] Hicks, *Value and Capital*, chapter 11.

[10] Speculators as well as hedgers can be on either side of the market. The large speculators are likely to be on the side opposite from the strong hedging interests. It is impossible to say which side the small speculators are likely to be on, though the question—while interesting—does not appear to be quantitatively significant.

One thing that can be said about small speculators is that they are not likely to stay for a long time on whichever side they are on. Typically they enjoy the idea of closing out a winning position quickly and while they are likely to bear a losing position as long as they can (until the loss becomes sufficiently large to drive them out of the market), that is often not too long. Some 85 percent of speculators lose money: of that 85 percent many follow this prescription for losing it—others find equally good prescriptions.

to borrow in local currencies, *ceteris paribus*. Empirical evidence appears to support these expectations.[11]

Owing to the difficulty of predicting distant-term spot prices of currencies, speculators would probably use a trend of past spot prices to help form an estimate of the spot prices likely to prevail in the distant future. Since the trend of past spot prices is likely to vary according to when one begins, many trends of past spot prices would in effect exist. The trends examined would be the long-term ones, since such data would be considered to be useful in making estimates of distant-term prices. An average of these trends would then be employed to help form an estimate of the future spot price (abstracting from possible policy and structural changes).

This averaging process would serve to mitigate fluctuations in the prices of distant-term futures contracts and would help to explain why the prices of distant-term currency futures would typically fluctuate less (often much less) than the prices of near-term currency futures. It does in fact explain why the prices of intermediate-term futures prices do typically fluctuate less than the prices of near-term futures contracts. It also helps to explain why futures prices—near-term and intermediate-term—typically underpredict the magnitude of future changes in spot prices.[12]

In addition to the term structure of futures premiums, there is a risk structure. The currencies that are considered to be unstable will have higher futures premiums (discounts) than the more stable currencies. Similarly, the commodities that are expected to have relatively unstable prices will have greater "backwardations" than those expected to have more stable prices. High bid-asked spreads will typically be associated with the high risk premiums.

The relatively high cost of speculation in some currencies and in the distant maturities of all currencies has contributed to an absence of contracts in many currencies and in all distant maturities. For the same reason, the intermediate-term maturities, where they exist, are

---

[11] Bankers have informed me that firms prefer to hedge by borrowing in the local currency rather than by using the forward currency market, *ceteris paribus*. Only if facilities for borrowing in the local currency are unavailable do some firms turn to the forward currency market. On this point, see the comments of Dennis Weatherstone and Geoffrey Bell at the AEI—Treasury Conference on Exchange Rate Flexibility, April 20-22, 1976. For commodity futures, the risk premiums embedded in forward rates correspond exactly in nature to those embedded in long-term interest rates. Cf. Hicks, *Value and Capital*, p. 147.

[12] I have examined ninety-day forward currency prices and the magnitude of subsequent (or future) changes in spot currency prices over a two-year period under floating rates. The data indicate that the ninety-day forward prices consistently underpredict the magnitude of subsequent (or future) changes in spot prices.

likely to be characterized by small open positions and fairly wide futures gaps. Such forward markets are therefore characterized by high (direct) costs of hedging. The futures gaps of intermediate-term maturities are, in effect, a situation between the low-cost futures gaps of some near-term maturities and the prohibitive-cost futures gaps of the distant maturities.

Unlike the commodity futures markets, where a large number of speculators of all sizes can be found (including the in-and-out group of M.D.'s who are continually feeding the markets), the forward currency markets have been limited primarily to the large speculators. As Burtle has pointed out, banks typically have wished to service only their business accounts, the apparent reason for this being the high cost of servicing small accounts, including the cost of involuntary defaults.[13]

For a while, commercial banks took extensive speculative positions in forward currency markets. However, bank failures and large foreign exchange losses by Herstatt, Franklin, Lloyds, and Banque de Bruxelles have restrained their speculative interest in this area.[14] In addition, the recent monitoring of bank foreign exchange positions by the U.S. Treasury and the bank regulatory agencies may also have served to restrain their speculative activity.

A large speculative interest in the forward (or futures) markets is, however, important, since it serves, *inter alia*, to reduce the cost of hedging—both the futures premiums and the transactions costs—by providing a balance to a market characterized by unequal hedging strengths.[15] Speculation also helps to improve the accuracy with which current futures prices predict future spot prices.

In the commodity futures markets, the "normal backwardation" (or, stated differently, the "average backwardation") described by Keynes will always persist.[16] In these markets, the hedgers are predominantly the producers of staple raw materials, all of whom are

---

[13] See James Burtle, "American Multinational Enterprises and the Emergence of Floating Rates: An Analysis of Changing Private Sector Roles and Strategies," presented at the annual meeting of the International Studies Association, Toronto, Canada, February 1976.

[14] Ibid.

[15] Because the volume of speculation in forward currency markets is likely to be smaller than the volume of speculation in commodity futures, the cost of hedging is likely to be higher, *ceteris paribus*. This point is in reference to the institutional constraint, not to the point made earlier in connection with note 11 to this chapter. Interest arbitrage will help to constrain the hedging cost in currency futures. It does not, however, determine the magnitude of hedging cost through the forward market, for reasons discussed earlier.

[16] Cf. J. M. Keynes, *Treatise on Money* (New York: Harcourt, Brace, and Co., 1930), volume II, pp. 142-44.

on one side of the market—namely, the demand side for forward contracts. In the currency futures market, the situation is different. Hedging demand will typically occur from both sides of the market, although (also typically) the strength of the hedging demand will be greater on one side of the market than on the other. Furthermore, the relative strengths of the hedging demands are not likely to change too quickly.[17]

Thus, in the currency futures market, the "backwardation" ("forwardation") can appear on either side of the market, and can change from one side to the other at any time. When there are strong hedging interests on both sides of the markets, the backwardation (forwardation) can move back and forth (forth and back), the only factor stopping it from moving beyond a certain point being the introduction of speculation when it becomes sufficiently profitable for speculators to enter the market.

There has been a lot of recent discussion as to whether a bias exists in the forward currency market. A number of economists have in fact examined the relationship between current forward rates and the corresponding realized spot rates for different currencies. With the preceding comments in mind, we must interpret these studies carefully. Hedgers may be changing their net position during the course of the period being investigated, and (as a result) so may speculators. In the currency futures markets (or forward markets), the futures "premiums" may be changing to "discounts," or vice versa. It depends on the degree of stability of the relative hedging interests. As indicated earlier, I would not expect the strength of relative hedging interests to switch too frequently (a point to be discussed shortly).

Thus, one cannot say that speculators have made money in one segment of a time period and lost money in another segment, inasmuch as the assumption that they have retained a given type of open position throughout the period is not necessarily correct. Indeed, they may have made money in both segments (or lost money in both segments). For any given period, speculators may be expected to lose money primarily from unforeseen events, and perhaps occasionally from lack of sufficient foresight. (The latter, if it occurs, would probably take place in a little-used market.) One must remember that speculators can have imperfect foresight and still make money.

---

[17] In an insightful footnote, Hicks stated, "This congenital weakness of the demand side of course applies only to forward markets in commodities, and will not apply (for instance) to forward markets in foreign exchange. However, in all forward markets there is likely to be a tendency for hedgers to predominate on one side or the other over long periods. No forward market can do without the speculative element." (Hicks, *Value and Capital*, pp. 137-38.)

Evidence on relative hedging demands over time would help to determine whether speculators were in fact making money. For many bilateral relationships, the strong hedging interest may be on one side of the forward currency market for a very long time, in which case speculators would then be on the other side for a very long time. This situation is likely to occur frequently in the relationship between a developed and developing country. In the case of two developed countries, this situation occurs less frequently. In fact, not only may the relative strengths of the hedging interests be more volatile, but the structure of hedging interests at a given time may be such that for some maturities the stronger hedging interest occurs from one side, whereas for other maturities the stronger hedging interest occurs from the other side. Indeed, there may even be more than one "cross" in the maturity structure of relative hedging strengths. For the more distant maturities, the relative strengths of the hedging interests should be more stable.

In the past, most hedging in the forward currency market involving the U.S. dollar has been done from only one side of the market—from U.S. investors wishing to hedge the expected economic exposure of their nonmonetary assets situated abroad (an expected long position in local currency).[18] To do so, they would take a short position in a forward foreign currency. However, for a combination of reasons, relative hedging strengths in the forward currency market appear to be changing. As will be pointed out in section 4 below, the new accounting standards have served to reduce the volume of short hedging positions in foreign currencies for a given volume of investment by U.S. multinationals. In addition, as is also pointed out, the new accounting standards have probably decreased the volume of new investment abroad, thereby reducing still further the volume of short hedging positions in foreign currencies. Furthermore, foreigners are increasingly turning to the United States for their investments. In part, this is a result of the increased availability of Arab oil money. Other countries, however, also appear to be investing more in the United States, as a result, perhaps, of increased confidence in the strength and stability of the dollar—which in turn may well be attributable to recent and prospective Federal Reserve policy.[19]

---

[18] Cf. Burtle, "American Multinational Enterprises and the Emergence of Floating Rates." Also, see note 17, above.

[19] U.S. monetary policy is likely to be steadier in the future than in the past, *ceteris paribus*, for at least two reasons: (1) the recent congressional mandate for money supply guidelines and (2) the recent inception of a futures market in Treasury bills and GNMA mortgages.

2. Hedging under Fixed and Floating Rates

During the calm periods of fixed rates, there was little cost in being exposed. As a result, multinationals often preferred not to hedge their exposed positions, especially for short periods of time, believing that the cost of hedging was not worth the benefit (namely, the reduction in the cost of exposure). Furthermore, in some situations—with an exchange rate expected either to remain fixed or to move only in one direction—the multinationals did not believe that there were any benefits to be realized from hedging an exposed position. (Alternatively, multinationals did not believe that there was any cost of being exposed.) In fact, many firms in such situations may well have considered an (appropriately) exposed position to be advantageous.

This writer is not suggesting that multinationals engaged directly in speculative activities under fixed rates; rather, they did it indirectly by, at times, leaving their balance sheets exposed in an appropriate way, given the market's prices, actual and expected economic conditions, and their estimates of the appropriateness of the relationship between prices and conditions. The fixity of exchange rates, in effect, enabled companies at times to engage in one-sided indirect speculation.

Thus, indirect speculation was, in effect, a by-product of commercial activities by firms that had little or no incentive to hedge during the calm periods of fixed rates. During crises, the multinationals did seek to hedge because of their uncertainty about the magnitude of possible rate changes. But it was precisely during these periods that the traditional sources of foreign exchange typically became unavailable, thereby rendering hedging extremely costly in time and money, indeed prohibitively so for many firms. In particular, the increase in uncertainty about the magnitude of possible rate changes served to increase the elements of hedging cost: the transaction costs and the futures premiums. Furthermore, during these periods, the increased possibility of governmental imposition of ad hoc exchange controls served to increase (often greatly) the cost of hedging. Indeed, the increase in the cost of hedging was typically greater than the increase in the benefit from hedging.

Under floating rates, a firm's cost of being exposed and its cost of hedging do not gyrate in the way that they do under fixed rates, where there are wide differences between calm and crisis periods. Under floating rates, the cost of being exposed over distant maturities is less than under fixed rates because of the expected smaller variation in rates for given underlying economic conditions (including government policies). Indeed, as Milton Friedman pointed out, real adjustments are continually being made in response to changes in exchange rates rather than being postponed as typically occurs under fixed rates, thereby necessitating eventual larger real adjustments through eventual larger changes in exchange rates.[20]

Under floating rates, we would expect the cost of distant-term hedging—the distant-term futures gap—to be lower (probably much lower) than under fixed rates. The primary reason is the probable smaller uncertainty attached to the expected future spot rate (realized). The reduction in distant-term hedging cost is, however, not apparent because this hedging cost is still prohibitive. (It is interesting to note the formal equivalence of this situation to a corner solution.) For intermediate-term hedging, if the cost is lower under floating rates than under fixed rates, the cost reduction should be reflected in a lengthening of maturities and an increase of open positions. Dennis Weatherstone of Morgan Guaranty Trust Company of New York has in fact informed me that—in his opinion—the maturities have been extended and a greater volume of forward hedging has occurred under floating than under fixed rates.

Over short periods of time, the cost of exposure and hedging under floating rates may often be somewhat larger than under fixed rates,[21] but these costs will also be more stable. It is likely that the

---

[20] Milton Friedman, "The Case for Flexible Exchange Rates," in idem, *Essays in Positive Economics* (Chicago: University of Chicago Press, 1953). Also, cf. Harry G. Johnson, "The Case for Flexible Exchange Rates," in George N. Halm, ed., *Approaches to Greater Flexibility of Exchange Rates: The Burgenstock Papers* (Princeton: Princeton University Press, 1970).

[21] *Ceteris paribus*, we would expect near-term bid-asked spreads as well as near-term futures premiums to be greater during the current floating rate system than they were during the fixed rate system. Also, however, we would expect distant-term bid-asked spreads as well as distant-term futures premiums to be lower during the current floating rate system than they were during the fixed rate system.

Many economists have recently noted that the bid-asked spreads have been greater during the current floating rate system than during the previous fixed rate system. Undoubtedly, part of the explanation is that the *ceteris paribus* assumption does not apply: instability in underlying economic conditions has been greater during the current floating rate system than during the previous fixed rate system (taken as a whole). However, it should also be noted that, in all the studies I have seen, the bid-asked spreads examined have been for futures contracts with a maturity of a year or less. Thus, the findings are not surprising. What is important, however, is that appropriate qualifications be placed on these findings so that they do not mistakenly lead to incorrect assessments of the desirability of floating rates.

Ronald McKinnon has collected some extremely valuable data on bid-asked spreads in his paper, "Floating Foreign Exchange Rates 1973-74: The Emperor's New Clothes" (mimeographed, November 1974, and to appear in this or a later draft in *The Carnegie-Rochester Conference Series*, vol. 3). The appendix to the paper presents data on the bid-asked spreads in the spot and futures markets from 1972 through 1974. All the spreads appear to have increased from 1972 to 1974. McKinnon notes that the bid-asked spreads in forward markets—particu-

switch to floating rates will result in an increase in the cost of near-term hedging that is smaller than the increase in the cost of near-term exposure, thereby leading to an increased volume of near-term hedging. If this happens, the principal reason might be the well-developed near-term forward markets that have attracted considerable speculative interest.

3. Uncertainty (Initial and Residual) under Fixed and Floating Rate Systems

It should be remembered that the switch to floating rates caught many multinationals (and many business schools) by surprise. Neither the cost of exposure nor the cost of hedging are household words; and when they are discussed, it is often done in a household manner.[22] For this reason, the effects predicted may not occur immediately. Indeed, there is a learning process on the way of life under floating rates that multinationals (and business schools) must undergo.

In making comparisons between business experience under fixed and under floating exchange rates, it is important that we keep in mind the nature of the periods being investigated, inasmuch as wide differences may exist in underlying economic conditions. In this connection, changes in underlying economic conditions during the recent floating rate period—resulting, *inter alia*, from changes in government policy and from the oil crisis—have probably been greater than those that occurred during most of the Bretton Woods period.[23] In fact, under the Bretton Woods regime, the only period comparable to the

---

larly on longer-term contracts—have risen more sharply than those in spot markets.

These data on forward contracts relate to time periods of one year or less, so that all contracts fall under the category of "near-term" futures contracts. If we look at the maturity structure of the bid-asked spreads, we find that the more distant-term contracts have wider bid-asked spreads. Although the spreads on the longer-term contracts did in general increase more in an absolute sense than those on the nearer-term contracts, they did not generally increase more in a relative sense: the percent increases in the bid-asked spreads on nearer-term contracts were in general larger than those on the longer-term contracts. This latter point seems to me the most relevant for our discussion here.

[22] See the survey of foreign exchange risk management practices of U.S. multinational corporations recently conducted by Professor Michael Jilling (especially question 16). A statistical summary of the survey's findings is contained in an Appendix to Alan Teck's paper, "International Business under Floating Rates," presented at the AEI—Treasury Conference on Exchange Rate Flexibility, April 20-22, 1976.

[23] Cf. Charles Pigott, Richard Sweeney, and Thomas Willett, "Some Aspects of the Behavior and Effects of Flexible Exchange Rates," presented at the Conference on Monetary Theory and Policy, Konstanz (Germany), June 1975.

recent period under floating rates may well have been the period leading up to and including the breakdown of the old regime. During that period, the fixed rate system could not cope with the divergences in government policy that brought floating rates into existence. And it should be remembered that the fixed rate system never even had to cope with the problems generated by the oil crisis.

For two reasons, the switch to floating rates appears to entail a reduction in distant-term uncertainty. First, the cost of distant-term exposure, as mentioned earlier, is likely to be lowered. Second, the cost of distant-term hedging is also likely to be reduced, although, as mentioned earlier, such cost reduction is not apparent for the distant maturities. The cost reduction is, however, apparent for the intermediate-term maturities, as was pointed out.

The effect of the switch to floating rates on near-term uncertainty is not unambiguous, since it depends on the type of period under fixed rates that we are considering—calm period or crisis period. On average, calm periods during the Bretton Woods regime did predominate, but the sample may not necessarily have been a representative one. In any case, if we compare the experience under the Bretton Woods regime with what the experience under floating rates would have been during the Bretton Woods years, we can reach some conclusions. The existence of floating rates would probably have entailed a greater cost of near-term exposure as well as a greater cost of near-term hedging than the costs that in fact existed under the fixed rates. For both reasons, near-term uncertainty would probably have been higher under floating rates during the Bretton Woods years than that which actually existed under the fixed rates.

To complete the analysis of near-term uncertainty, however, we would have to compare the experience under floating rates during the recent period with what the experience under fixed rates (adjustable peg) would have been. With a large degree of instability—either from large changes in government macroeconomic policies or from large abrupt changes originating in the private sector—near-term uncertainty is likely to be less under floating rates than under fixed rates. In the past, such instability under fixed rates occurred infrequently, lending skepticism to the belief that near-term uncertainty is likely to be less under floating than under fixed rates. It must, however, be remembered that a large degree of instability in the past has typically been associated with a breakdown of the fixed rate system; and that such instability was not (and could not be) cured overnight by floating rates. Just as it takes a considerable period of time with an unstable situation before expectations based on that instability are formed, so it takes a considerable period of time with a calm period before so-called normal expectations return.

Thus, if we can be assured of periods of relative calm, fixed rates would appear to entail a lower amount of near-term uncertainty than floating rates. But, in response to such a statement, Milton Friedman might say to his class, "if my mother had wheels, she'd be a bus." Indeed, the fact of the matter is that we are not living in a period of relative calm; and with national governments desiring independence in the formulation of domestic macro-policies, we are not likely to be living in such a situation for some time. Furthermore, as Harry Johnson has aptly stated, "a fixed exchange rate system is a fair-weather system."[24] The problem is that the weather can deteriorate very easily. Indeed, one major problem of a fixed system is its almost inevitable prospect of breakdown, since bad government policies are not recognized easily or quickly.

The market knows when a government is pursuing inappropriate policies, and the market will try to punish the currency in question accordingly. Under fixed rates, however, the government often seeks to mask the poor quality of its policies by treating disturbances with ad hoc measures. In response to the depletion of reserves, swaps are arranged and, if necessary, trade and exchange controls are instituted. The government can try to tell the people that the problems are short-term disturbances (undoubtedly "caused by speculators") but such assurances will be futile unless the government adopts a more responsible policy.

Under floating rates, when the government begins to pursue inappropriate policies—such as an unwarranted increase in the rate of monetary expansion—the market will also react, but the effects of the reaction will be different from the effects that occur under fixed rates. The exchange rate falls, rather than reserves being depleted or ad hoc measures being imposed. Furthermore, if a continuation or even acceleration of the monetary excesses is anticipated, speculators may sell the currency in far greater amounts than the initial expansion of money supply would appear to justify. As a result of these actions by speculators, the international value of the currency in question may drop precipitously.

Policy officials are concerned about the international value of their currency and look at its value many times every day. Seeing the precipitous fall in their currency's international value, they will try to determine the contributory factor(s); and if they discover the rea-

[24] Harry G. Johnson, "World Inflation and the International Monetary System," *The Three Banks Review*, no. 107 (September 1975), p. 5.

son(s), which should not be a difficult task, they may take corrective measures. A learning process might ensue. One hopes that policy officials would recognize the long-run cost of a too-rapid monetary expansion and would not tend to repeat the scenario.[25]

In the scenario sketched above, speculators would have been responsible (in a proximate sense) for shifting the exchange rates around. Furthermore, the swings in exchange rates would not have had a good correlation with changes in economic variables. And yet the speculators would be performing a useful social service.

Many economists, including Edward Bernstein, have been studying whether the recent swings in exchange rates could be justified by underlying changes in the national economies.[26] Various data have been examined—prices, money supplies, interest rates, and so on. The scenario depicted suggests that we must be cautious in the way we interpret these data. It also suggests that speculation under a floating rate system is more likely to provide a built-in stabilizer than it is under fixed rates.[27]

It is paradoxical that speculators, whom the government is always trying to thwart, are typically performing a useful social purpose. It is also paradoxical that speculators are seldom hurt by governmental measures designed to thwart their money-making ability. Indeed, speculators probably made more money under the adjustable peg system than they are making under floating rates. It is rather the multinationals that are hurt by governmental ad hoc measures, in part because they do not have the flexibility that the speculators possess.

In conclusion, the switch to floating rates thus appears to entail a reduction in distant-term uncertainty, with an increase in near-term uncertainty in certain situations and a decrease in near-term uncertainty in others. For this reason, floating rates would appear to favor

[25] Unfortunately, however, policy officials might react to a fall in the international value of their currency in a different way. They might seek to use some or all of the paraphernalia—the ad hoc measures—that they used during the crisis periods of the Bretton Woods regime. As pointed out later, this could have serious consequences for a system of floating rates. This writer in fact expects policy officials initially to follow the route of the ad hoc measures, as exemplified by the recent loan to Great Britain. Only after such measures continually prove to be useless—as will inevitably happen unless they are accompanied by a more responsible government policy (in which case the measures would be unnecessary, except for a possible short-run effect or for a perverse desire to be subjected to control by other countries)—is there any hope, in this writer's view, for a relatively clean float and for a well-functioning international monetary system.

[26] E. M. Bernstein, "Two Years of Fluctuating Exchange Rates," *Report no. 75/7* (Washington, D.C.: E M B Ltd., April 12, 1975).

[27] On these points, cf. Harry G. Johnson, "World Inflation and the International Monetary System," especially pp. 5, 11-12, and 15-16.

long-term international investment, whereas fixed rates would appear to favor (perhaps only in a comparative-advantage sense) international commercial interests.

The important (and perhaps excessive) economic and political position of commercial interests (especially commercial banks, acting directly as well as through their respective central banks) in the leading industrial countries as well as the customary (but unwarranted) suspicion of international investors and speculators may thus help to explain why the adjustable peg system of fixed rates persisted for so long.

Paradoxically, in the long run, even the commercial interests may be favored by floating rates. The increased rate of economic growth and development throughout the world (resulting from the higher rate of investment) would induce an increased volume of international commercial business. Stated differently, the fixed rate system, through its neglect of long-term international investment, might well lead eventually to a lower volume of international business than would occur under floating rates.

4. Implications of New Accounting Standards for Multinationals

As was indicated earlier, *Statement No. 8* has introduced a new element into firms' decision making. For many firms, the discrepancy between accounting exposure and economic exposure has been greatly increased. This increased discrepancy has created severe problems for some firms. Previously, the concern of the multinationals had been directed primarily at the EEE (expected economic exposure) of their assets and liabilities. Now, however, their attention to the EEE has been diverted to some extent, in many cases to a great extent, by their attention to the EAE (expected accounting exposure).

The increased discrepancy between the EEE and EAE of many multinationals has, in effect, decreased the demand for hedges of economic exposure. In particular, as was indicated earlier (Chapter 2, section 3), those firms that had not been using the monetary–nonmonetary standards have sought to alter—at least partially—their new EAE; but in so doing they have typically also altered their planned economic exposure. The usual result has been an increase in the net long EEE, as well as an increase in the net short EAE (either from what it was in the situation before *Statement No. 8* or from what it would be in a situation of economic value accounting).

Previously, firms were concerned primarily with their economic hedging. Now, however, under *Statement No. 8,* they are concerned about accounting as well as economic hedging (as was pointed out in Chapter 2, section 3). In effect, the benefits of economic hedging have been reduced. As a result, the demand for economic hedging has been reduced by many firms, leaving a larger exposed economic position.

Furthermore, unlike the earlier situation under fixed rates, where the multinationals' speculation was indirect (in the sense that it was a byproduct of commercial transactions), the recent speculation is direct. It does not, however, have the same motive as direct speculation in the usual sense of the term.

Previously (Chapter 3, section 2), we had noted that there is a reasonably stable demand for hedging exposed positions under floating rates. The stability of this (economic) hedging demand is likely to be affected by *Statement No. 8*. Because of the new accounting considerations, the demand for economic hedging (as well as accounting hedging) is likely to be more variable than it was previously. Corporate managers and directors are likely to vacillate in the relative importance that they attach to the effects of the accounting distortions and the costs of adjusting thereto. Furthermore, the effects of the distortions as well as the costs of adjustment will be altered over time, as a result of changes in the economic environment and of possible accounting-induced alterations in the firm.

One final point should be made. To evaluate business experience under floating rates, it is important to isolate the effects of *Statement No. 8*. Otherwise, the findings (and implications) of empirical studies might well be biased against floating rates.

5. Implications for Government Policy

The U.S. government may become concerned about the increased speculative positions—economic and accounting—of multinationals, occasioned by *Statement No. 8*. This concern may prompt the government to impose regulations on the activities of multinationals.

Governmental actions designed to curb (economic or accounting) speculation by multinationals will in fact impinge on the hedging (and "hedging") adjustment mechanism of firms. And governmental actions that curb the use of any adjustment mechanism will throw the burden of adjustment on the remaining mechanisms. The residual mechanisms would be required to adjust to an increased volume of hedging. Hedging might well be distorted towards real hedging, because governmental restrictions are likely to fall initially on financial adjustments. In any case, the cost of hedging adjustment would probably increase.

An increase in the cost of hedging adjustment would be extremely unfortunate. Recently, considerable discussion has been directed at determining the reasons for the large changes in exchange rates that have occurred under floating rates. Little attention by policy officials appears to have been focused on the way firms cope with exchange rate volatility. Under floating rates, hedging is the lifeblood of multinationals.

This paper has pointed out how firms seek to reduce their economic exposure, but are unfortunately constrained to some extent by the new accounting standards. They have increased the cost of doing business for multinationals under floating rates. If the cost of hedging adjustment were increased still further by governmental actions, the viability of multinationals might be seriously threatened.

This suggests that governments should be mindful of regulations such as exchange and capital market controls that have an important bearing on the hedging adjustment ability of multinationals. It is not clear that governments ever consider such effects when they are formulating such regulations.[28]

Under floating rates, U.S. capital and exchange controls—such as OFDI regulations, interest equalization taxes, and short-term capital controls—have been removed. The increased freedom of capital movements has enhanced the flexibility of the adjustment method, thereby allowing multinationals increased flexibility in managing their exposure. Any movement by the United States in the opposite direction (resulting from any factor such as fears about OPEC), which in turn may induce foreign retaliation, is fraught with far graver consequences for the viability of international trade and investment than would be the situation under fixed rates.

---

[28] Cf. Dufey, "Corporate Financial Policies and Floating Exchange Rates." This is not to say that governments show no interest in multinationals. Consider for example, the intensive discussion now taking place on a code of conduct for multinationals—a response to the widespread corrupt-practices scandals recently uncovered. Unfortunately, however, governments typically do not show a similar concern for the operating problems of multinationals. Furthermore, in this writer's view, the governments' concern over the recent bribery disclosures has not appeared to be entirely equitable. This is not to say that any exoneration should be given the multinationals—clearly their conduct was reprehensible. However, it should be remembered that there is a demand for as well as a supply of corrupt practices. At least equal concern should be addressed to the demand side of the equation. And I am not here referring simply to the narrow issue of the individual politicians who may be guilty. Rather, I am asking what gives foreign politicians the ability to extract such bribes. Asking questions such as this and seeking answers thereto would help get at the source of the problem rather than merely focusing attention on its symptoms. I hope that the appropriate foreign governments will address their deliberations to this broader issue as well as to the narrower one.

4

CONCLUDING OBSERVATIONS

As this paper has pointed out, *Statement No. 8* of the Financial Accounting Standards Board has created some serious problems for multinational firms. Corporate managers have been induced to make wrong (nonoptimal) business decisions and the ability of corporate directors to control their firms has been impaired. In addition, there have been some adverse effects on the national economy and the international economic scene. The effects have in fact become so adverse that some multinationals are considering the possibility either of using alternative standards of translation for certain assets or of seeking an exemption through the SEC from certain aspects of the FASB's ruling.

The use of alternative standards would necessitate a qualified opinion by a firm's auditors. Most corporate directors are at present opposed to having such an opinion. In all likelihood, this opposition is based in part on possible adverse security market effects for the firm. Of much greater significance to the corporate directors may be the firm's "public image," which is a factor (indeed an important factor) affecting the public's demand for governmental regulation of multinationals in general or of the director's firm in particular.

A widespread seeking of exemptions through the SEC would raise some ominous clouds. The SEC could in effect overrule the FASB, but in doing so it might not merely negate the specific FASB rulings, but might also seriously weaken an already embattled FASB as a private rule-making authority. Certainly, it is far from clear that public rulings on accounting standards would be superior to private rulings. For this reason, *inter alia*, it is essential that the FASB's recent ruling (*Statement No. 8*) be judiciously evaluated.

As was pointed out (Chapter 2, section 4), the new standards have created some serious economic problems. Investment by multinationals is likely to have been curtailed and the allocation of resources for a given volume of investment distorted. In addition, a bias has been created against floating rates (Chapter 3, section 4). This bias is unfortunate in view of the greater benefits that multinationals realize under floating than under fixed rates (Chapter 3, sections 1–3). Nevertheless, this paper has also pointed out that the new system, with its uniformity of treatment, may—in certain respects—be preferable to the old system that permitted numerous standards to exist simultaneously (Chapter 2, section 4).

The real problem is not with *Statement No. 8*. Indeed, as this paper has noted (Chapter 1, section 3), the new standards are not capricious, but—taken as a whole—are rather carefully based on generally accepted accounting principles. The real problem is with the generally accepted accounting principles. In particular, the use of historical cost accounting for certain balance sheet items has created discrepancies between accounting data and the economic values they are attempting to describe (Chapter 2, sections 1 and 2). And it is these discrepancies that create serious problems for firms (Chapter 2, sections 3 and 4). The magnitude of these discrepancies has increased in our current environment of inflation and price uncertainty.

In this writer's view, the FASB was right in bypassing the issue of the appropriateness of generally accepted accounting standards in *Statement No. 8*. If the generally accepted accounting principles are to be changed, they should presumably be changed for all firms— domestic as well as multinational.

If one takes the generally accepted accounting principles as given, no single method of translation and hence no accounting standards would be satisfactory for all multinationals. Serious effects would have occurred no matter which accounting standards were adopted. The only difference would be in the number and specificity of firms adversely affected. This conclusion logically follows from the great diversity among firms in the exposure of their nonmonetary assets (whether on a realized or expected basis). The fact that a method of translation similar to the one adopted was apparently being used more frequently than any other method suggests that the decision reached was probably the best way of achieving uniformity, given the generally accepted accounting principles.[1]

In view of the problems caused by historical cost accounting for the balance sheets of firms—domestic as well as multinational—a

[1] Cf. Financial Executives Institute, Committee on Corporate Reporting, Foreign Exchange Conversions Subcommittee, "Survey of U.S. Company Foreign Translation Practices," October 1973. A summary of this survey was printed in *Financial Executive*, vol. 41, no. 12 (December 1973).

comprehensive examination of generally accepted accounting principles would appear to be urgently needed. Such a review is in fact currently being carried out by the FASB in its wide-ranging study of accounting objectives and principles.

The quality of the balance sheets of firms has long been neglected not only by accounting boards but also by the firms themselves.[2] Indeed, it is somewhat paradoxical, though also quite fortunate, that business firms—many of which had seriously neglected the quality of their balance sheets for years (which neglect, as we know, recently culminated in a large number of bankruptcies and severe liquidity problems)—are now clamoring for reform of outmoded accounting standards.[3]

The introduction of economic value accounting (current value accounting, with an adjustment by a general price index where appropriate) appears to be the only way of mitigating the problems arising under existing accounting standards. Such a standard would indeed eliminate the discrepancies that exist today between accounting data and economic values. In so doing, it would encourage corporate managers to make correct (optimal) business decisions, and would enhance the ability of corporate directors to control the operations of their companies. It would also remove the existing accounting-induced bias against investment of all kinds, but particularly with respect to long-term, capital intensive projects. In addition, it would remove the bias that has been created against floating rates.

There has been some discussion to the effect that economic value accounting would not eliminate the volatility of multinationals' earnings. This is indeed true: earnings will be volatile for any one of several reasons, including the volatility of exchange rates. Economic value accounting would, however, reduce the unwarranted, incremental volatility of earnings that exists under *Statement No. 8*.

Economic value accounting is not, however, immune from problems. Many difficult conceptual and measurement problems would exist under such a standard. For example, there are many different measures of current value—such as replacement cost, exit (or sale) value, and value to the specific firm—and each of these measures is likely to give a different result (perhaps a very different result) from that given by the other measures.

These practical problems are in fact the primary reasons why historical cost accounting for some items has persisted for so long. Other reasons may include the possibility that firms may abuse cur-

---

[2] See "Focus on Balance Sheet Reform," *Business Week*, June 7, 1976, pp. 52–60.
[3] Ibid.

rent value accounting measures by shopping around for the "best value," and the possibility that certified public accountants may become subject to more lawsuits under current value accounting, where elements of judgment perforce replace mechanical calculations, than they now are.[4]

The practical problems entailed in the use of economic value accounting are, to be sure, numerous and difficult, but they do not appear to be insurmountable. Recently, the SEC ruled that large firms—beginning in 1977—must disclose estimates of replacement cost of inventories and fixed assets (productive capacity) in footnotes to reports filed with the SEC. This ruling, as the SEC itself acknowledged, is an experiment. The crucial issue is whether the benefits from this experiment (in the form of increased information) outweigh the costs involved—not simply the direct costs to firms in added paperwork, but also and more importantly, the indirect costs to firms from the loss of confidence that may arise if reporting requirements are continually changed. This experiment may turn out to be a costly one.

In its wide-ranging study, the FASB is currently wrestling with the practical problems entailed in the use of current value accounting. The element of time favors a shift to economic value accounting: continuing inflation and price uncertainty augment the cost of existing standards. Indeed, as was stated earlier, living as we are in an age of uncertainty, it would be preferable to have figures that are reasonably accurate rather than to continue the use of figures that are assuredly wrong. The first country that adopts economic value accounting standards is likely to become the Texas or Delaware among nations. Other countries will be induced to follow suit.

One final comment is worth making. Economic events and accounting standards are inextricably related. Economic events help shape accounting standards, which in turn affect economic events.

Indeed, the clamor for and the inception of accounting standards were probably a response to the increased complexity of economic events that increased the cost of being without standards. Certainly, uniform accounting standards for multinationals were a reaction, *inter alia*, to the increased volume of international investment and the increased volatility of exchange rates, which allegedly increased the cost of having numerous standards simultaneously in existence. And the recent clamor for realistic accounting standards is certainly a

---

[4] Cf. Howard J. Trienens and Daniel U. Smith, "Legal Implications of Current Value Accounting" in *Financial Executive*, vol. 40, no. 9 (September 1972), pp. 44-77.

reaction to the persistence of inflation and price uncertainty that have increased the economic cost of existing standards.

Accounting standards should not, however, be viewed merely as passive elements on the horizon of economic events. Rather, they affect and shape economic events, as this paper has in fact demonstrated. If too rigid, the standards may impede economic progress. I hope that the setting of standards can be sufficiently flexible so as to respond in a constructive way to economic events and thereby help to foster sound business policies.

APPENDIX: SUGGESTIONS FOR EMPIRICAL RESEARCH

Several research areas would appear to be fruitful for testing implications of points made in this study. Let me briefly mention a few research areas in Chapter 2 as well as offer some suggestions about the methodology that might be employed in such research.

Adjustment Methods and Costs

Several implications of this study may be explored. For example: (1) What changes in the method(s) and magnitude(s) of hedging adjustments did the new standards appear to induce? (2) Is there an association between the type of firm (for example, manufacturing, marketing) and the method or magnitude of adjustment, and if so, what may have accounted for such an association? (3) Is there an association between the capital structure of a firm and the adjustment method(s) and magnitude(s) used? (4) Is there an association between a firm's diversification and the adjustment method(s) and magnitude(s)? (5) How prevalent is the accounting "hedge"? (6) Is there an association between the nature and magnitude of adjustment and the country (countries) where the subsidiary (subsidiaries) is (are) located? (7) Is there an association between the standards previously chosen and the cost of adjustment?

To answer such questions, data about firms could be grouped according to which firms had opted for the monetary–nonmonetary method and which had not. For the latter group, data compiled before and after January 1, 1976 (with perhaps a consideration of possible short-run trends leading up to January 1, 1976) would be helpful in providing answers to a number of questions that may be raised about adjustment methods and costs. Also, countries could be grouped according to how stable their currencies have been. And firms could be grouped according to differences in industrial classification, differences in capital structure, and differences in effective diversification.

Security Markets

Several implications of this study may be explored. For example: (1) Was there a difference in the security market evaluation of firms that had been using the monetary–nonmonetary method and those that had not? (2) Has there been a difference in the market's evaluation of firms that had not opted for the monetary–nonmonetary standards and new firms of a similar nature? (3) For the firms whose EAE was altered, did the market distinguish between them according to the location of a subsidiary, the type of subsidiary, or the capital structure of the subsidiary? Indeed, many of the same questions raised above in connection with adjustment method(s) and magnitude(s) can be raised here.

To answer such questions, we could group firms according to which had opted for the monetary–nonmonetary method and which had not. In looking at security markets, we would not expect to find the pronounced shifts on or around January 1, 1976, that we would expect to find in the studies on adjustment method(s) and magnitude(s). The reason is that the security markets anticipate events as well as react to them. In fact, it is only the unanticipated events that may be expected to have a pronounced effect on security markets.

In this connection, we should keep in mind that many of the security market implications of the new standards may have been felt long before the actual change went into effect. Before January 1, 1976, there had been the issuance of a *Discussion Memorandum,* the issuance of an *Exposure Draft,* and the issuance of *Statement No. 8.* We must also remember that discussions on the subject were occurring prior to the issuance of the *Discussion Memorandum.*

Of the three documents, the *Exposure Draft* may well have had the largest short-run impact on the security markets. The issuance of *Statement No. 8* should also have had an effect on the market through the elimination of uncertainty.

In gathering security market data for the type of groupings among firms that was suggested earlier, we would want to look at both price-earnings ratios and borrowing costs.

Exposure

Several implications of this study may be explored. For example: (1) Did the firms that had not opted for the old monetary–nonmonetary standards have a relatively large volume of short-term or long-term debt denominated in a foreign currency? (2) Is there an association between the standards previously chosen and the magnitude of expected economic exposure now existing? (3) Is there a tendency for firms to be established with the same type of economic exposure that typically exists for firms which had opted for the old monetary–nonmonetary standards?

To answer such questions, we could group firms according to which had opted for the monetary–nonmonetary standards and which had not. To secure the appropriate information, an examination of corporate balance sheets and interviews with corporate treasurers would be necessary.

Cover and book design: Pat Taylor